Networks in Contention

How do civil society organizations mobilize on climate change? Why do they choose certain strategies over others? What are the consequences of these choices? *Networks in Contention* examines how the interactions between different organizations within the international climate change movement shape strategic decisions and the kinds of outcomes that organizations are able to achieve. First, it documents how and why cleavages emerged in this once-unified movement around the time of the 2009 Copenhagen Summit. Second, it shows how an organization's position in the movement's network has a large influence on the tactics it adopts. Finally, it demonstrates how the development of new strategies within this network has influenced the trajectory of global climate politics. The book establishes the ways in which networks are consequential for civil society groups, exploring how these actors can become more effective and suggesting lessons for the future coordination of activism.

JENNIFER HADDEN is an assistant professor in the Department of Government and Politics at the University of Maryland. Her research on such topics as international relations, environmental politics, social network analysis, and social movements has been published in *Mobilization* and *Global Environmental Politics*. In 2012, she was the co-recipient of the American Political Science Association's Virginia M. Walsh Dissertation Award for the best dissertation in the field of science, technology, and environmental politics. She also received the 2011 Esman Graduate Prize for Distinguished Scholarship from Cornell University and a Young Scholars in Social Movements award from the University of Notre Dame in 2010. She is a regular participant in the UN climate process.

Cambridge Studies in Contentious Politics

Editors

Mark Beissinger, *Princeton University*

Jack A. Goldstone, *George Mason University*

Michael Hanagan, *Vassar College*

Doug McAdam, *Stanford University and Center for Advanced Study in the Behavioral Sciences*

Sarah Soule, *Stanford University*

Suzanne Staggenborg, *University of Pittsburgh*

Sidney Tarrow, *Cornell University*

Charles Tilly (d. 2008), *Columbia University*

Elisabeth J. Wood, *Yale University*

Deborah Yashar, *Princeton University*

Books in the Series

(Continued after the index)

Networks in Contention

The Divisive Politics of Climate Change

JENNIFER HADDEN

University of Maryland, College Park

CAMBRIDGE
UNIVERSITY PRESS

CAMBRIDGE
UNIVERSITY PRESS

32 Avenue of the Americas, New York, NY 10013-2473, USA

Cambridge University Press is part of the University of Cambridge.

It furthers the University's mission by disseminating knowledge in the pursuit of education, learning, and research at the highest international levels of excellence.

www.cambridge.org
Information on this title: www.cambridge.org/9781107461109

© Jennifer Hadden 2015

First published 2015

Printed in the United States of America

A catalog record for this publication is available from the British Library.

Library of Congress Cataloging in Publication Data
Hadden, Jennifer (Jennifer Leigh)
Networks in contention : the divisive politics of climate change / Jennifer Hadden, University of Maryland, College Park.
    pages   cm. – (Cambridge studies in contentious politics)
Includes bibliographical references and index.
ISBN 978-1-107-08958-7 (Hardback : alk. paper)   1. Climatic changes–Political aspects.   2. Climatic changes–Social aspects.   I. Title.
QC903.H185 2015
363.738'74–dc23   2014043066

ISBN 978-1-107-08958-7 Hardback
ISBN 978-1-107-46110-9 Paperback

To my parents, Eileen and Lyall, for everything

Contents

Figures

Tables

Acknowledgments

Climate change is the greatest challenge of our times. This book documents the ways in which civil society actors have tried to address it. I want to acknowledge the assistance of the many activists, advocates, and policy makers who gave their scarce time to participate in this project. During my research I was routinely impressed with their dedication and creativity in the face of immense global problems. I hope that I do them justice in explaining their actions and motivations. This research could not have happened without them.

I began research for this book in the summer of 2007. My work was initially motivated by a desire to study protest on climate change – something that was still mainly embryonic at that point. I ended up focusing much more on what I observed activists actually doing: negotiating the consequential relationships that produce collective action in the first place. This has proven to be a rich and rewarding topic of study. Much of this research was conducted during my time as a graduate student in the Department of Government at Cornell University. At every stage, I have benefited enormously from the support and mentorship of Sidney Tarrow. Sid's pathbreaking work on these topics has been a continuing inspiration for my own research. I am immensely grateful for his insight and generosity.

Elements of this research have been presented at a number of conferences and workshops. The resulting work has been greatly improved by suggestions from numerous discussants, panelists, and audience members. I would particularly like to acknowledge those that provided me with feedback on draft versions of these chapters, including Chris Anderson, Josh Busby, Sarah Bush, Scott Byrd, Charli Carpenter, Jeff Colgan, Donatella della Porta, Mario Diani, Matt Evangelista, Janice Gallagher, Jessica Green, Michael Heaney, Lorien Jasny, Doug McAdam, David Meyer, Tsveta Petrova, Ruth Reitan, Chris Rootes, Lucia Seybert, Jackie Smith, Sarah Soule, Suzanne Staggenborg, Sarah Stroup, Stacy VanDeveer, Wendy Wong, and Andrew Yeo. The insightful comments I received from these scholars, and countless others, have undoubtedly improved my work.

I received generous support for this project from a number of institutions. I conducted full-time field research from June 2008 to December 2009, culminating with the 2009 Copenhagen Summit. This immersion was made possible by the financial support of a Fulbright Fellowship to the European Union and a Haas Dissertation Fellowship from the European Union Studies Association. I particularly wish to thank the Climate Action Network Europe for its hospitality during this time period. The Institute for Social Sciences, Center for European Studies, and Center for a Sustainable Future at Cornell University provided me with invaluable opportunities to conduct additional field research trips outside of this time period. My continued research on this topic and attendance at international climate change conferences have been supported by the College of Behavioral and Social Sciences and the Department of Government and Politics at the University of Maryland, as well as the National Socio-Environmental Synthesis Center.

My colleagues at the University of Maryland have been especially generous in supporting my work. I owe particular thanks to Dana Fisher, Virginia Haufler, Mark Lichbach, and Shibley Telhami, who read the entire book and offered many valuable suggestions for improvement. Isabella Alcaniz, Kanisha Bond, David Cunningham, Nate Hultman, Scott Kastner, and Joel Simmons also offered insightful comments on key points. I have benefited from the skilled research assistance of Joan Chu, Kim Cullen, Marques Gillham, Devon Howard, Neda Movahed, Kate Richards, Maria Sharova, Emilee van Norden, and Felipe Westhelle.

I thank my editor at Cambridge University Press, Lew Bateman, for his support of this undertaking, as well as the anonymous reviewers for their thoughtful comments. Linda Benson and Kristy Barker greatly improved this manuscript with careful editing. Some of the material in this book was previously published in *Global Environmental Politics*. I thank MIT Press for permission to reproduce it here.

I am grateful to have had steadfast support from my family and friends during the research and writing of this manuscript. I dedicate this book to my parents, Eileen and Lyall Hadden, in recognition of their innumerable contributions. Laura Hadden and Jesse Friedman unfailingly encouraged my efforts and made me laugh at countless points. Scott Frick read and carefully commented on many chapters of the manuscript. My interaction with these wonderful people makes my work more enjoyable, and I am grateful for their love and support.

Washington, D.C.
July 2014

Introduction

It was a bright and unseasonably warm winter day. People streamed into Copenhagen by early morning to participate in an event billed as the "Global Day of Climate Action." It was a big success. The crowd snaking through the streets approached 100,000 at its peak. Protesters held signs that read "There is no Planet B" and "Bla Bla Bla ... Act Now!" to reference the urgency of the ongoing climate negotiations. The sun had set by the time the protesters reached the venue of the climate summit. The crowd assembled in the dark, illuminated by the glow of candles as Desmond Tutu led a vigil for climate protection. Speaker after speaker beseeched world leaders to act on the critical challenge of climate change. Individuals in the crowd linked arms and sang songs of solidarity.

A very different scene was unfolding simultaneously across town. While the "family-friendly" march was making its way toward the venue of the conference, approximately 2,000 individuals fell behind. Many of these activists formed their own bloc to march separately from the rest of the protesters. They distinguished themselves by wearing black clothes and bandanas. A few broke off to smash windows and spray-paint buildings as they began to leave the downtown area. The Danish police responded by arresting more than 700 individuals that morning. Many of those arrested were made to sit on the sidewalk for more than five hours. Those that were not arrested continued their march, holding banners proclaiming "change the system, not the climate" and "climate justice now!" They linked arms, closed ranks, and maintained their distance from the other marchers assembled in front of the venue, drumming and chanting for climate justice from a site about half a mile away from the other activists.

This event, in Copenhagen in 2009, was the moment at which the world anticipated a successor agreement to the Kyoto Protocol. Environmental organizations were expected to be there. Civil society participation at previous conferences had been managed by mild-mannered, scientifically sophisticated nongovernmental organizations (NGOs). But it was already clear by November that Copenhagen was going to be very different. The head of police issued a warning stating that "violent extremists" were likely to target the summit. The panicked Secretariat of the United Nations Framework Convention on Climate Change (UNFCCC) issued a set of participation rules – typeset in bold, capital letters, in red ink – that expressly forbid "unapproved protest actions" in the venue. The UN Security Team began to realize that more than 10,000 activists, some of whom had made explicit threats of radical action, would have access to a venue housing world leaders. An atmosphere of tension and nervous anticipation pervaded the first week of the negotiations.

The final week of the conference was a descent into chaos. The negotiations among parties were falling apart over issues of mitigation targets and equity. The mainstream NGOs were working night and day to try to influence states and to apply pressure to ensure the best deal possible. But more radical groups had already threatened to engage in direct action and Seattle-style summit protests to take over the talks in Copenhagen, all the while ramping up activity in the streets. Security forces responded to activists with preemptive arrests, tear gas, and beatings. The panicked Secretariat reacted by banning observers almost completely for the final three days. This resulted in both conventional and contentious organizations being shut out of the conference – an unprecedented move in the history of the UNFCCC.

The negotiations collapsed days later, producing a nonbinding accord that fell dramatically short of expectations.

Copenhagen was a highly consequential conference in the history of climate governance. It was also a conference that was marked by an unprecedented level of contentious activism. How did all this activism come about, and why did it take the forms that it did? This book shows that it emerged from two related, but largely independent, components of a massive transnational civil society network.

On the one hand, transnational NGOs working inside the UN negotiations organized numerous actions and media stunts during Copenhagen to build support for their concrete negotiating positions. They anchored their demands in available climate science, using numbers such as "350" or slogans such as "Keep Global Warming Below 2 Degrees!" They painstakingly built the world's largest transnational advocacy network – composed of 700 NGOs in more than ninety countries – to lobby decision makers for enhanced climate protection.

In parallel to these efforts, another cohort of activists came to Copenhagen to mobilize along entirely different dimensions. These activists were well versed in the politics of the global justice movement and had experience protesting international meetings of the World Trade Organization (WTO), the International Monetary Fund (IMF), and the G8. They built a coalition that bridged the issues of the global justice movement and climate change, using a broader slogan – Climate Justice Now! – to attract a more radical constituency. Critically, they convinced other prominent organizations and individuals to go along with their approach, building support for a justice-based issue framing and introducing a repertoire of radical action into the politics of climate change.

The meeting of these two organizing models meant that civil society organizations within this network faced critical choices: either they could continue to work on an inside track, using primarily conventional tactics and a science-based framing, or they could move to the outside, radicalize their approach, and adopt a justice-based framing.

Groups took opposing – and sometimes unexpected – paths in negotiating these choices. This book explains how they made these decisions. In doing so, I detail how civil society organizations have mobilized historically on climate change, how their strategies have changed over time, and how the interaction between actors in this arena has shaped their decisions. It also tackles difficult questions about the implications of this activism for the politics of global warming and for the future of international climate change governance.

THE PUZZLE

It is not enough to know that there was ample protest in Copenhagen. We want to know *why* protest emerges and *how* it matters. The analysis in this book looks closely at how organizations make tactical choices regarding forms of collective action, to explain why so many of them adopted contention in Copenhagen.

Actors do not go out and simply act collectively. They use a variety of specific action forms – protests, pickets, or petitions, for example – from a broader repertoire of collective action to try to influence their targets (Tilly 1978, 151; Tarrow 2011, 39). These choices are critical to civil society organizations. Groups weigh their tactical options seriously and are acutely aware that they must ultimately face the reputational consequences of their decisions.

Despite the importance of these tactical choices to the actors making them, this is a subject that scholars know surprisingly little about. As Jeff Goodwin and James Jasper (2004, 16) observe, "the actual choice of actions from within the repertoire – not to mention issues of timing and style in their application – has been almost completely ignored." Interest group scholars Frank Baumgartner and Beth Leech (1998, 165) echo this assessment, stating "our review ... convinces us of two things: groups engage in a wide variety of lobbying tactics, and scholars have yet to explain how they choose among those tactics."

When scholars do tackle this issue, they tend to study either conventional forms of action, such as lobbying, or contentious forms of action, such as protest. As David Meyer (2004, 137) notes, we know little about the choice between the two, and "the relationships among different types of activism are also begging for more empirical work." Aseem Prakash and Mary Kay Gugerty (2010, 18) lament that the existing NGO literature cannot "explain how and when NGOs decide to use 'insider' versus 'outsider' strategies ... or the decisions of some NGOs ... to reorient their strategies."

How do we explain why some actors decide to adopt contentious forms of collective action, while others do not? Scholars have offered two general explanations. First, political process theorists argue that organizational behavior should respond to changes in the external political opportunities available for participation. For example, research in this tradition has argued that actors' behavior should become more contentious when opportunities for participation become more limited (Meyer and Minkoff 2004; McAdam 1999; Tilly 1978; Tarrow 2011).

While political process theory makes an important contribution to this topic, it is limited in its ability to explain the choices of individual actors. It may be perfectly correct that when opportunities are reduced, more actors choose protest. But virtually every movement has variation in the forms of action that are employed at any given time. What about those that do not respond to political opportunities, protesting when opportunities are abundant or continuing to try to lobby when access is scarce? Many actors in my study subvert the general expectations of political opportunity theorists. How can we explain their behavior?

Organizational theorists help with this problem. This work shows how an organization's ideology, structure, and resources can influence its tactical choices (McCarthy and Zald 1977; Piven and Cloward 1977; Dalton 1994). From this vantage point, the behavior of advocacy organizations should respond to both their normative and instrumental concerns (Prakash and Gugerty 2010; Keck and Sikkink 1998). For example, we should expect organizations that are older and have more resources to be less contentious, and those that have more radical ideological orientations to tend toward more contentious forms of action.

Considering organizational factors helps explain why changes in political context do not affect all actors equally. But this approach is more limited in its ability to explain organizational change. Scholars working within this tradition tend to consider change unlikely (Hannan et al. 2006), develop simple stage theories that predict unidirectional change (Michels 1958), or essentialize organizations and their ideology (Dalton 1994, 209). But many actors in my study changed their forms of action during the time period in which I observed them without significantly altering their other attributes. How can we explain these changes? And, more specifically, how can we explain which actors will change, and why?

This book argues that both political process and organizational theories are important in explaining organizational choices, but both overlook the importance of *relationships* in organizational decision making. This book develops a network approach to collective action that helps explain who adopts contentious forms of action, and why they do so.

THE NETWORK APPROACH

My network approach is situated in relational thinking. Relational thinking differs from the traditional approaches to collective action in that it considers organizational decisions to be interdependent. This means that knowing the structure of relationships between organizations can be as important as understanding the properties of organizations themselves or the characteristics of the political system in which they operate (see Mische 2010; Emirbayer 1997).

Relationalists are concerned with what Mark Granovetter (1985, 482) calls the problem of embeddedness: "that the behavior and institutions to be analyzed are so constrained by ongoing social relations that to construe them as independent is a grievous misunderstanding." To say that actors are embedded in relations places the focus on the social ties that allocate resources, information, and meaning differentially across populations of actors. In this view, social structure emerges from stability in patterns of relations among actors. In turn, the structure of these relations both empowers and constrains the choices of the individual actors.

This perspective reveals the limitations of studying advocacy organizations as analogous to firms (Prakash and Gugerty 2010). While this approach illustrates the importance of organizational structure and incentives, it underplays the importance of relationships between organizations. Advocacy organizations self-represent to members, funders, and the media as independent units with unique brands (Barakso 2010). But in most instances, they must also cooperate and compromise with other groups to advance their causes. Networks "soften the boundaries of organizations" by facilitating the exchange of information, resources, and meaning (Lecy, Mitchell, and Schmitz 2010, 242). There is nothing contradictory in this duality: the network perspective allows us to understand how civil society can be composed of both instrumentally motivated organizations and a network of principled advocates.[1]

The relational approach integrates elements already present in other approaches to social movement studies. For example, the relational approach draws on the original insight from political process theory that political opportunities have to be perceived in order for them to affect choice of tactics (McAdam 1999, x). Similarly, it highlights the resource mobilization insight that it is not individually held but collectively mobilized resources that matter for generating collective action (Edwards and McCarthy 2004, 114). But it goes beyond both of these approaches by highlighting which elements of explanation are properly relational. It also explains apparent empirical contradictions by systematically theorizing how social relations influence important political outcomes.

---

[1] Organizations are very conscious of this duality. As one interviewee explained to me regarding the strategy of the international climate coalition: "We work together quite a lot. But we know that we all represent different brands, so we have to be careful to give the appearance of not working together all the time" (Interview, WWF European Policy Office 2008).

Relational theorists consider both individual behavior and collective outcomes to be the product of interdependent actions of members of the system (Coleman 1986). Thus, methodologically, relationalists often use different approaches – qualitative and quantitative – to consider the role of interdependence in generating individual choice and social outcomes. Social network analysis is one way to implement a relational approach (see Diani and McAdam 2003), although network analysis and relationalism do not always perfectly overlap (Emirbayer and Goodwin 1994).

Drawing on the tradition of social network analysis, this book emphasizes that patterns of interorganizational relations influence organizational strategic decisions. Networks influence an organization's choice of action form because they can encourage tactical harmonization between closely connected groups. In other words, I expect organizations to adopt contentious forms of action when their peers have already done so. I find that this is true in the time period I study, even after controlling for other important factors.

Why would organizations harmonize with their peers? My research emphasizes the importance of three mechanisms. First, networks structure an organization's relationships with other organizations, thereby facilitating *information sharing*. As a result, an organization's position in a network may provide it with information about opportunities or choices that it otherwise might not be aware of (Ansell 2003). Information sharing can spread knowledge about the planned tactics of other organizations, aiding in determining whether a particular collective action proposal will meet the threshold at which it is likely to be successful (Granovetter 1978). Finally, information sharing can also stimulate interorganizational learning about tactics that leads to the adoption of new forms of action. For example, Wang and Soule (2012) find that collaboration is an important channel of interorganizational tactical diffusion among American social movement organizations.

Second, network ties can facilitate *resource pooling*. Resource pooling is important because it can help an organization overcome its individual resource limitations. Through resource pooling, an organization can draw on not only its own resources but also the resources of others for purposive action (Lin 2001). Organizational coalitions are often created as permanent vehicles for resource pooling between participants (see Bandy and Smith 2005; McCammon and Van Dyke 2010). For example, Diani, Lindsay, and Purdue (2010) find that diverse social movement coalitions in Bristol and Glasgow share both material and symbolic resources, regardless of the type of collective action they organize.

Third, groups may also use *social influence* to persuade one another of the utility or desirability of certain tactics. This influence can function directly, convincing others to change their plans for action as a result of negotiation or discussion, or it can function indirectly, convincing organizations to change their underlying identities and in turn implying different forms of collective action. For example, Taylor and Whittier (1993, 118) use the history of the lesbian feminist movement to suggest that "groups negotiate new ways of thinking and acting" that can change both their identities and forms of action.

Understanding how relational mechanisms operate is important for developing a more complete knowledge about the dynamics of collective action. My documentation of the operation of relational mechanisms in this book helps establish their importance in organizing collective action and, in turn, in influencing the nature of climate politics.

ARGUMENT OF THE BOOK

This book is organized around four key arguments. In combination, they help us understand why Copenhagen was so contentious, why some organizations adopt contention and others do not, and how this matters for climate politics. Figure I.1 summarizes the structure of the argument.

First, the expansion of political opportunities changed the population of the organizations that mobilized on climate change. More organizations began to work on the topic as

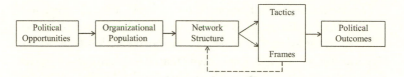

FIGURE I.I. Structure of the Argument

climate change became a more salient issue. As the nature of climate negotiations became more complex, a more diverse group of organizations – representing environmental NGOs, development NGOs, global justice organizations, and radical social movements – all began to participate in climate politics.

Second, changes in the organizational population resulted in the emergence of a divided network. The network became less connected as the population of organizations became larger and more complex. Groups began to form different coalitions to compete with one another. This resulted in a divided network with two main components: groups engaging in conventional climate advocacy and those adopting a contentious climate justice approach. The two sides of this network rarely communicated or coordinated collective action in Copenhagen.

Third, network structure influenced the tactics and framing choices of civil society organizations. Civil society groups are embedded in a network of ties with other groups. These ties influence the decisions that they make because organizations share information, pool resources, and influence one another to adopt similar forms of collective action and collective action frames. Divisions in the network meant that some organizations were exposed to organizations already using contentious tactics while others were not, helping to explain differential adoption of tactics. The choices organizations made in turn also contributed to the restructuring of the network as organizations built new coalitions and alliances in advance of Copenhagen and in the years after.

Finally, the tactics and frames used by civil society groups influenced political outcomes. We would not be interested in civil society activism if we did not think that it was important.

This book demonstrates three ways in which civil society activism is consequential for the politics of climate change. First, as groups' actions in Copenhagen became more contentious, the UNFCCC introduced more restrictions on civil society participation. Second, the climate justice frame developed by civil society groups spread to the media and to important parties in the negotiations. Third, the analysis and strategies of civil society groups contributed to a new cleavage in international politics, adding to the turbulence in the negotiations in Copenhagen.

This is not to say that activism changed everything. Activists were still far from achieving their ultimate objectives in Copenhagen. But it did change the political process in important ways that are perceptible in hindsight. Examining the scope and pathways of influence in Copenhagen suggests ways in which civil society groups may reorient their coordination and target their activities for future rounds of climate negotiations.

PLAN FOR THE BOOK

This book documents a transnational network of civil society groups, its operation, its effects on actors within it, and its collective influence during an important period of climate policy making. This is no easy task. Collecting data on international networks is notoriously difficult on its own. Although the importance of networks may seem intuitive, it is often challenging to detect their influence empirically, given the plausibility of a number of observationally similar alternative explanations (Hafner-Burton, Kahler, and Montgomery 2009; Ward, Stovel, and Sacks 2011).

I respond to the complexity of this task by developing a multimethod research strategy that integrates multiple data types at different levels of analysis. I combine social network analysis, quantitative historical analysis, statistical analysis, content analysis, qualitative interviewing, and participant observation to support my central claims. I rely on extensive original data collection, both qualitative and quantitative. This includes eighteen months of fieldwork with civil society organizations in 2008 and 2009.

I incorporate different data and analysis for each chapter of the book, as this section details. The careful design of this research ensures that the multiple data types complement one another and should make the reader confident in my findings. I try to avoid technical detail in the text whenever possible. I invite the interested reader to consult the detailed Methods Appendix for more information about the data collection and analysis employed in this book.

The structure of the book is as follows. Chapter 1 provides important political context by explaining why the time period of this study – from 2007 to 2009 – was such a crucial moment for international climate change negotiations. Drawing on media analysis and coding of institutional records, I argue that two important changes in civil society participation occurred during this time. First, the growing salience of the climate issue drew a large number of organizations to work on the topic, many for the first time. Second, the increased complexity of the negotiations led a more diverse population of organizations to become involved with the issue. Thus, by the time of the conference in Copenhagen, climate politics was no longer the exclusive province of environmental NGOs but also included the participation of development groups, youth groups, and transnational social movements.

In Chapter 2, I use social network analysis to explore how changes in the organizational population affected the structure of relations among groups. I argue that the network became less connected as the population of organizations expanded and diversified. I draw on membership lists from international climate change coalitions to construct the network of actors in 2006 and 2009. I show that by the time of Copenhagen, the network had become highly divided between those organizations adopting the strategy of conventional climate advocacy and those taking a more confrontational climate justice approach. Qualitative interviews suggest that these network divisions affected the network's ability to facilitate communication and collective actions around the Copenhagen meeting.

Chapter 3 addresses the question of how organizations make tactical decisions. I argue that an organization's position in the network has an important influence on its choices. Specifically, I find that when organizations have ties with other organizations already using a contentious strategy, they are more likely to adopt contentious approaches themselves. This finding holds even after taking into account the characteristics of the political environment and the organization's attributes. I argue that this relationship is driven by relational mechanisms of information sharing, resource pooling, and social influence. I also suggest that these mechanisms explain why we see protest spread among closely connected actors in social networks.

I make this argument by analyzing an original dataset of a group of civil society actors that mobilized on climate change in the European Union from 2008 to 2009. I built this dataset in three phases. First, I identified all the relevant transnational collective actions on climate change in the European Union during this time period. Next, I analyzed hundreds of documents to identify the sponsors of these actions, allowing me to construct a network of actors based on event co-sponsorship. Finally, I coded these organizations' Web sites to document their attributes, including resource profile, ideology, and size. I analyze these data using network and statistical analysis.

Chapter 4 presents a case study of those organizations in the network employing conventional advocacy strategies. I detail the development of network ties among these groups, their science-based approach to framing the climate change issue, and the motivation for their selection of conventional advocacy strategies. I also highlight how the power and social influence of major actors – such as Greenpeace and the Climate Action Network – promoted the conventional advocacy approach and convinced other groups to resist pressure toward tactical radicalization.

Chapter 5 complements Chapter 4 and looks at organizations that decided to adopt a strategy of contentious activism. I show how initially a small set of organizations in the network decided to reframe the climate change issue in terms of broader justice

issues and adopted a risky outsider protest strategy inherited
from the global justice movement. I document how these organizations reached out to new groups, sharing information, pooling
resources, and eventually persuading others – including major
NGOs such as Friends of the Earth – to adopt a similar approach.
This resulted in the rapid diffusion of the protest strategy within a
certain portion of the network and the emergence of a high level
of contention in Copenhagen.

Both Chapters 4 and 5 rely on extensive qualitative data that
I collected during my fieldwork in 2008 and 2009. I conducted
more than ninety organizational interviews, observed 200 hours
of organizational meetings, and collected hundreds of organizational documents. My analysis of the qualitative data lends
support to the correlations I observe in the quantitative
analysis.

Finally, Chapter 6 explores the implications of civil society
activism for global climate change politics. I suggest several
pathways through which civil society groups are able to
achieve broader influence. I draw on coding of media reports,
state speeches, and NGO newsletters to document how the
climate justice issue framing was picked up by a wide variety
of actors, demonstrating the framing power of civil society.
I show how the use of climate justice language supported a
new and consequential cleavage in international climate
change negotiations. I also document how the use of contentious tactics has stimulated a process of institutional reform
within the UNFCCC that has thus far not worked to the
advantage of activists.

I conclude by briefly summarizing the contributions of the
book and reflecting on broader issues. This book demonstrates
that the network approach could be usefully employed to
enrich our understanding of the alliances and cleavages
that characterize an increasingly complex global civil society.
Lessons learned from this case – especially those concerning
diversity and the need for deliberation – could be useful to those
concerned about the future of governance within civil society

networks and in international institutions. In light of strategic discussions being held in advance of the 2015 climate negotiations, I suggest that civil society groups can maximize their influence by strengthening their networks, building new connections and bridging the gaps between organizations working in this sphere.

I

The Copenhagen Moment

The UN Climate Change Conference in Copenhagen was the moment at which world leaders expected to develop a successor agreement to the Kyoto Protocol. The meeting attracted an enormous amount of attention in popular media and political debate. As the *New York Times* summarized:

The massive interest in the meeting seemed a measure of rising expectations that negotiators will find their way to some sort of agreement or set of agreements – even if it's short of a treaty – that will render the meeting a success.

"Within two weeks from Monday, governments must give their adequate response to the urgent challenge of climate change," said the United Nations climate chief, Yvo de Boer, in a statement on Sunday. "Negotiators now have the clearest signal ever from world leaders to craft solid proposals to implement rapid action."

(Zeller 2009)

The growing salience of the issue attracted a large number of civil society organizations to the world of climate politics from 2007 to 2009. The population of groups involved in this issue expanded dramatically within a short period of time. But changes in the substance of the international negotiations also increased the diversity of organizations. Groups from a wide variety of issue backgrounds – including international development, women, youth, indigenous peoples, and the global justice movement – all began to refocus their work around the topic of climate change in advance of this meeting.

This chapter explains how the population of civil society groups working on climate change has expanded and diversified in response to changing political opportunities. I do this by linking the history of civil society participation to developments in international climate change politics in each major period of the negotiations between 1998 and 2012. I draw on institutional records and organizational interviews to document these connections. I show that the increased turbulence in international negotiations was echoed and amplified by disagreements and divisions among civil society groups. Thus, this chapter not only explains these important transformations in the population of civil society groups but also sets the stage for the analysis of the rest of this book.

GROWING PARTICIPATION IN CLIMATE CHANGE POLITICS

Climate change is an ecological process caused by an increase in the release of greenhouse gases (GHGs) into the atmosphere as a result of human activity such as burning fossil fuels and deforestation. These GHGs are heat-trapping; as their density in the atmosphere increases, they warm the planet and cause changes in the climate. Scientists suggest that these resulting changes can have a number of harmful consequences, including drought, sea-level rises, food shortages, increased severe weather, shortage of drinking water, and the extinction of a number of plant and animal species (Intergovernmental Panel on Climate Change 2013).

Though scientists have understood the phenomenon for decades, climate change was not always a high-profile policy issue. Much of the activism on climate change in the 1980s and early 1990s was concerned primarily with putting the issue on the international agenda. This goal was realized when the first international regime to address the issue – the United Nations

FIGURE 1.1. Number of Registered Observer Nongovernmental
Organizations to the UNFCCC
Source: United Nations Framework Convention on Climate Change
Participation Report (2013).

Framework Convention on Climate Change (UNFCCC) – was
created at the 1992 Earth Summit in Rio de Janeiro.

The UNFCCC has always sought to be inclusive of civil society
concerns. From its inception, it has had procedures in place for
civil society organizations to register to observe sessions of the
international climate negotiations, including the annual high-level
meeting commonly known as a "conference of the parties" (COP)
(Joachim and Locher 2008; Hoffman 2008). The number of organizations taking advantage of this opportunity has increased over
time. Figure 1.1 reports data from the UNFCCC's official participation report (2013) regarding the number of registered NGOs at each
COP (see also Schroeder, Boykoff, and Spiers 2012; Fisher 2010).

As these data show, participation of nongovernmental organizations has steadily increased from the first COP (1995) to COP
19 (2013). Initially, approximately 200 organizations registered.
This total grew at a steady pace to reach slightly less than 800 by
2005. The number of new groups in any given year ranged
between 30 and 100. But 2009 was a major exception. The
demand for participation exploded as 345 new organizations
registered to attend the Copenhagen Summit. This surge in new
registrations   brought   the   total   number   of   registered

organizations to 1,319, increasing the number of nongovernmental observers by about 35 percent in one year. Even more dramatically, the number of individuals registered as observers increased from about 4,000 in 2008 to over 13,000 in 2009.

Why did so many civil society groups decide to get involved in climate change politics in 2009? First, the media began to pay more attention to the topic. Research by Maxwell Boykoff (2013) documents media coverage of climate issues over time and shows attention increasing in national newspapers from 2006, peaking in 2009, and decreasing afterward. Many suggest that Al Gore's documentary *An Inconvenient Truth* (2006) helped spark a lot of interest and debate about climate change. Arriving after Hurricane Katrina and several devastating European heatwaves, the documentary connected the climate change issue to recent weather events in major developed regions.

Simultaneously, scientists began to highlight the urgency of the climate problem. The Intergovernmental Panel on Climate Change's (IPCC) Fourth Assessment Report (2007) claimed not only that climate change was happening faster than had been expected but also that the consequences would be more severe. The report indicated an increased certainty among scientists that the causes of global warming are anthropogenic. The IPCC report made it clear that ambitious action was needed by the year 2020 to avoid the most dangerous impacts of climate change. By awarding Al Gore and the IPCC the Nobel Peace Prize in 2007, the Nobel Prize Committee (2007) drew even more attention to the issue. The combination of increased media attention, growing scientific certainty, and the simple reality that the effects of climate change were becoming more apparent and threatening to citizens all over the world contributed to increased demand for organization.

Political factors were also crucial. The impending expiration of the Kyoto Protocol meant that parties to the UNFCCC had to begin negotiating a successor agreement during this time period. The decision was made to finalize the new treaty by the time of the 2009 meeting in Copenhagen, making this the crucial deadline. International donors began to step up to provide more money for advocacy on the topic.

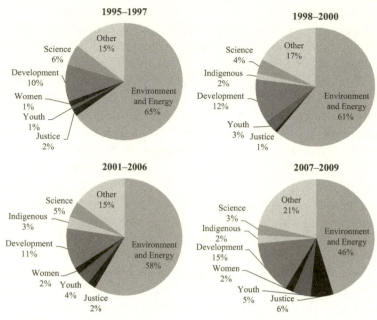

FIGURE 1.2. New NGO Registrants to the UNFCCC, by Issue Focus
and Year
Source: Data adapted from Muñoz Cabré (2011).

These factors alone could explain the increased participation.
But the story is more complex. Not only did more organizations
become involved in climate politics from 2007 to 2009, but the
types of groups involved also became more diverse. The UNFCCC
participation report (2013) also offers evidence of this change.
Miquel Muñoz Cabré (2011) coded the participation report
through 2009 to categorize NGOs registered with the UNFCCC
by the primary thematic category of their work. I draw on his work
in Figure 1.2 to show how the issue focus changed over time.[1]

---

[1] I slightly modified Cabré's dataset to exclude business and research organizations. I also combined categories to better visualize the data. Specifically,
I coded environment and conservation, energy, climate change, forests, water,
oceans and fisheries and built environment as "environment and energy" issues.
I included sustainable development and development in the category of "development" and listed remaining groups outside the science, women, youth, indigenous, and justice categories as "other."

These data show that environmental NGOs have been the primary participants in climate politics for most of the history of the UNFCCC. These groups constituted 65 percent of new registrants from 1995 to 1997, 61 percent from 1998 to 2000, and 58 percent from 2001 to 2006. But from 2007 to 2009, environmental NGOs comprised only 46 percent of the new registrants. They were still the biggest constituency, but far from the only type of organization involved. Groups representing development, justice, youth, indigenous, and women's issues also began to participate in the UNFCCC in larger numbers during these crucial years. Development and justice groups comprised 21 percent of the new groups, suggesting that this was an important new element in civil society.

Why did Copenhagen attract a more diverse crowd? Part of the answer may have to do with what Sikkina Jinnah (2011) calls "climate bandwagoning." Seeking attention from the media, donors, or members, civil society organizations working on a wide variety of topics – peacebuilding, human rights, and poverty, for example – all began to reframe their agendas to fit into the climate change area. Groups increasingly found that other environmental issues, such as deforestation, desertification, and biodiversity and fishery depletion, could be effectively reframed as byproducts of global warming. As one environmental activist explained it to me, "climate change isn't just an issue anymore, it's *the* issue, a meta-issue for everything we work on" (Interview, Danish 92 Group, 2009).

Another part of the answer has to do with the actual process of climate change itself. As the effects of climate change became increasingly real and threatening, many individuals already engaged in transnational activism were drawn to climate change organizing. Earlier history in transnational organizing – especially through the global justice movement – taught activists the benefits of developing multi-issue frames and of connecting individual issues to larger structural critiques (Smith and Weist 2012). The coalitions, email listservs, and interpersonal ties resulting from this wave of activism were an important resource that could be redirected toward climate issues when the timing was right (Hadden 2014).

But climate change politics also became much more complex during this time period. More actors had a stake in what was being discussed as issues such as international development, adaptation, climate finance, and carbon markets became a bigger part of the UNFCCC's agenda. To explain how the scope of the climate debate influenced civil society participation, the next sections detail the interaction between the political discussions and civil society participation in each major time period of the negotiations. In doing so, I hope to explain the political process by which the climate change issue transformed from one of narrow, technical concern to environmentalists alone to one of the "hottest" issues in the world.

PUTTING CLIMATE CHANGE ON THE AGENDA: 1988–1994

At first blush, climate change may seem like a difficult problem on which to mobilize. Given that many of the most dramatic effects of global warming are hypothesized to take place on a global level and in the distant future, the direct causal connection between emissions of greenhouse gases and global warming is unlikely to be observed by the average citizen. In other words, climate change is a difficult environmental issue because it requires the involvement of science (Sarewitz and Pielke 2000).

Thus, it is unsurprising that the early groups engaged on the issue were those with extensive scientific resources. The Earth Defense Fund had its scientific staff, Michael Oppenheimer in particular, writing opinion pieces on climate change as early as 1984. However, it was not until James Hansen's dramatic testimony before the U.S. Congress in 1988 that environmental groups began to show sustained interest in advocacy on the topic.

It was clear from the beginning that environmental groups were outnumbered and would need to work together to have a shot at successful advocacy. Starting in 1989, these organizations came together to form a coalition: the Climate Action Network (CAN). CAN was founded as a vehicle for transnational coordination among sixty-three organizations. As Michele Betsill (2000) documents in her study of the early years of CAN, those individuals participating in the original negotiations were much more academic than they were activist. Much of the early organizing on climate change came from advocates who had the technical capacity to digest scientific information. As one participant explained it, "At the beginning there was a lot of scientific information that was coming out. And it wasn't all sexy and 'save the whales.' It was technical, boring stuff" (Interview, Transport and the Environment 2009).

The fact that CAN had a strong scientific bent had important implications for how its advocacy developed. In the agenda-setting phase, NGOs contributed a good deal of their own scientific analysis to the political process. Many of the environmental NGOs involved during this time period had the capacity to perform scientific and policy research on topics related to accounting for greenhouse gas emissions (Rahman and Roncerel 1994). For example, Greenpeace published a scientific synthesis on global warming, the Stockholm Environment Institute began to work on targets and indicators of climate change, and the World Wildlife Fund (WWF) began to issue reports on the ecological impacts of climate change in the early 1990s. One of the earliest CAN joint projects was the "Escaping the Heat Trap" paper, which explicitly drew on the experience of the Montreal Protocol on ozone-depleting substances to propose ways to deal with the climate change issue (Betsill 2000, 169). As many of the early CAN participants had also been involved in the ozone negotiations, this analogy seemed apt.

The first big success for CAN was the signing of the UNFCCC at the 1992 Rio Earth Summit. The text of the UNFCCC (1992), which entered into force in 1994 after ratification by fifty countries, committed developed countries to reducing their GHG emissions to earlier levels. It also established the principle of "common but differentiated responsibilities" between developed and developing countries, an ambiguous phrase that nevertheless recognized uneven responsibility and capacity for emissions reductions.

The UNFCCC text did not, however, commit countries to concrete emissions reduction goals, as had the Montreal Protocol. The European Community clearly wanted to start negotiations on a protocol with binding targets and timetables immediately after the creation of the UNFCCC. But U.S. and Russian opposition stalled this effort until the election of Bill Clinton in 1993.

NEGOTIATING THE KYOTO PROTOCOL: 1995–7

The first COP to the UNFCCC took place in Berlin in March 1995. In what was known as the Berlin Mandate, delegates agreed to negotiate limits to GHG emissions for the post-2000 period. This was an opportunity for NGOs to deepen their engagement. Much of CAN's efforts promoted the work of the IPCC and helped establish its centrality in the international climate regime. As the CAN *ECO Newsletter* from the second COP in 1996 stated: "Ministers must take substantial decisions on the policy implications of the IPCC Second Assessment Report. Specifically, the key decisions would include: Adoption of [the report] as the most comprehensive and authoritative statement of scientific and technical knowledge on climate change ever produced" (Climate Action Network 1996).

CAN decided that all its political demands should be based on peer-reviewed science, a decision that was intended to high-light the coalition's scientific legitimacy in the face of climate change deniers. While other frames were theoretically possible, CAN drew on climate science and the conclusions of the IPCC to frame the climate change problem as a scientific issue that required an international policy solution. For example, the same newsletter also called for ministers to "negotiate a CO_2 emission reduction target that is ecologically justified and that will lead to stabilization of atmospheric concentrations of greenhouse gases well below 450 ppmv CO_2 equivalent" (Climate Action Network 1996).

Environmental groups also attempted to build support for action on climate change by painting it as a "crisis" that required urgent action (see also Busby 2010, 120). Environmental NGOs have taken this position since the beginning of negotiations in 1995, arguing in 1996 that "The requirement in the Berlin Mandate that negotiations on further emission commitments be conducted as a matter of urgency [has] not been honoured in practice. So far pitifully little has been achieved and governments risk failing to achieve the task they set themselves in April 1995" (Climate Action Network 1996). This frame of scientific urgency was routinely employed in position papers and lobbying documents at this time. This early advocacy set the tone for years to come.

The process of intergovernmental negotiations proved to be difficult. By the 1997 Kyoto Summit, it appeared as though the negotiations would fall apart over issues of national targets and emissions trading. The U.S. delegation challenged the EU proposal for equal reductions across developed countries and began to call for differentiation to take into account the unequal costs of adjustment. The United States also demanded that developing countries take on binding emissions targets, to much resistance.

The resulting Kyoto Protocol was the product of intense negotiation and compromise. The final Kyoto text (1997) did mandate an average reduction in GHG emissions of 5.2 percent below 1990 levels by developed countries, but to be shared unequally. The national targets under the Kyoto Protocol ranged widely: it called for an 8 percent increase for Australia, stabilization at 1990 levels for Russia, a 7 percent reduction for the United States, and an 8 percent reduction for the EU. It contained provisions not only for emissions trading but also for a clean-development mechanism and joint implementation projects. Both of these mechanisms allow developed countries to receive emissions reduction credits for financing projects that reduce emissions in developing countries. Developing countries were not required to take on binding targets. And while the outline of the agreement was in place, many of the details remained to be sorted out at future conferences.

THE DEVIL'S IN THE DETAIL: 1998–2000

Negotiating the Kyoto Protocol was only the first step. The text of the protocol stipulated that it could enter into force only after ratification by at least fifty-five states that were parties to the UNFCCC. In addition, the treaty needed to cover those states that were responsible for the majority of CO_2 emissions in order to be successful. Thus it specified a second condition that ratifications needed to be secured from parties representing at least 55 percent of CO_2 emissions in 1990. Although many developing countries ratified immediately (easily surpassing the fifty-five-party threshold), many industrialized countries held out to try to negotiate more favorable conditions and to hold sway in more technical discussions. Negotiators expected to finalize the Kyoto Protocol at the 2000 COP in The Hague, but political disagreements – particularly related to the operation of carbon markets – prevented this from happening.

In parallel, the first real test of internal unity in CAN came during the intense negotiations over the implementation of the Kyoto Protocol. As the climate change policy process moved from agenda-setting to negotiating concrete solutions, advocacy groups had to become increasingly specific in their proposals. This led to more disagreement among them. In particular, divides emerged in the network over policy issues related to carbon markets, coalition governance, north–south equity, and the use of disruptive tactics (Carpenter 2001). An equity caucus within CAN and a new group known as the Rising Tide Network began to question whether CAN's positions and tactics were too cautious. Many observers believed that the network might fragment at the 2000 meeting.

Equity was the biggest question. Reflecting on the meeting in The Hague, CAN leader Matthias Duwe (2001) suggests that there were four main sets of actors in this debate:

1. Northern environmental NGOs (many in the United States) that tended to be insensitive of north–south divides and called for equal sharing of the burden.
2. CAN leaders and big southern NGOs that called for equitable burdens for the common good.

3. Progressive northern NGOs and pragmatic southern groups that focused on calling for northern action before the south contributed.
4. Frustrated groups in the north and south that declaimed northern dominance and felt excluded from the discussion.

Duwe's analysis suggests that the second and third positions were the most numerous in the coalition. Yet it was clear that a group of dissatisfied actors (though small in number) viewed the network as a source of conflict and division. Moreover, this dissatisfaction was located on both ends of the political spectrum within CAN.

Despite these potential faultlines, leaders managed the disputes and the network remained cohesive. In fact, CAN consolidated its coalition structure during this period by creating a high-level political group to facilitate policy and strategic coordination among member groups. The resolution was only temporary, as subsequent years would show.

AMBIGUITY AND ENTRY INTO FORCE: 2001–6

By the 2001 COP in Marrakesh, it appeared as though considerable progress had been made on the operationalization of the Kyoto Protocol. The hope was that if Al Gore were elected, the United States would submit the protocol for ratification. These hopes were dashed when newly elected U.S. president George W. Bush announced in 2001 that he would not seek U.S. ratification of the protocol. Ratification was still mathematically possible without the United States, but it would require the participation of all members of the EU, as well as Canada, Japan, and Russia. By 2004, countries representing 44 percent of the developed countries' 1990 emissions had ratified. If Russia – which represented 17.4 percent of 1990 emissions – ratified, the treaty would come into effect. Ultimately, the EU agreed to support the Russian bid to join the World Trade Organization in exchange for Russian ratification. Thus, the Kyoto Protocol entered into force in February 2005 without the participation of the United States.

This was an ambiguous time for climate change advocacy. Many groups were angered by the U.S. withdrawal. Much climate activism assumed an anti-Bush tone and connected with the transnational mobilization of the peace movement. It was argued in some corners that NGOs had indirectly contributed to the U.S. failure to ratify by pushing up the ambition of the agreement. But the lesson everyone drew from Kyoto was that U.S. participation was key to the success of any future agreement.

This time period also offered an opportunity for reflection. A small group of organizations began to develop analyses opposing the use of carbon markets as a major policy mechanism for fighting climate change. Skepticism regarding carbon markets was once a widely shared principle in the environmental movement, but after the introduction of the flexibility mechanisms under the Kyoto Protocol, many mainstream environmental groups had come to grudgingly accept their use in an effort to stay relevant to the international negotiations. A number of groups remained opposed, however; some of these groups were anticapitalist in nature, while others simply rejected the system's operation in practice or its application to global pollution trading.

These critical positions were best summarized in the 2004 "Durban Declaration on Carbon Trading." The Durban Declaration spoke out against the neoliberal turn in climate politics, which it claimed leads to the privatization and commoditization of the atmosphere. As the document stated:

As representatives of people's movements and independent organisations, we reject the claim that carbon trading will halt the climate crisis. This crisis has been caused more than anything else by the mining of fossil fuels and the release of their carbon to the oceans, air, soil and living things ... We denounce the further delays in ending fossil fuel extraction that are being caused by corporate, government and United Nations' attempts to construct a "carbon market," including a market trading in "carbon sinks."

(Durban Group for Climate Justice 2005)

With this rejection of carbon trading, these groups positioned themselves far from CAN, and far from the reality of the political negotiations of the UNFCCC. As we will see, this became particularly significant in the leadup to Copenhagen.

DEBATING THE POST-2012 AGREEMENT: 2007–8

Almost as soon as Kyoto was ratified, states began to consider what would happen when it expired. The first discussions on this topic began in 2007. But the world had changed a great deal between 1997 and 2007. One of the biggest issues was that developing countries – especially China – were now major contributors to global carbon dioxide emissions. China surpassed the United States in its annual CO_2 emissions in 2006, although developed regions remain historically responsible for most of the CO_2 in the atmosphere. Developing countries had not been required to reduce their emissions under the Kyoto Protocol. But it was obvious by 2007 that any agreement that would fight climate change would need to secure support from developing countries.

The other major change in the negotiations was that negotiators had to face facts on climate adaptation. Negotiators in Kyoto had hoped to avoid climate change through international cooperation. It was clear by 2007 that some climate change was inevitable, and that international negotiations would be needed on both climate mitigation and climate adaptation. The first major step in this process was the development of the Bali Action Plan at COP 13 in 2007. The Bali meeting was generally considered the moment at which the blueprint for a future climate treaty would be determined.

The Bali Action Plan (2007) stipulated that delegates would negotiate a new treaty to succeed Kyoto by COP 15 in Copenhagen. The Copenhagen deadline was considered important because the Kyoto Protocol would expire in 2012, and the estimate was that states would need at minimum two years to ratify any new agreement. It also stated that any new text would require developed countries to give substantial aid to developing countries to support any mitigation and adaptation efforts that developing countries might undertake. As always, many issues were left open for discussion.

A whole new crop of civil society organizations began to get involved in climate change politics during this time period. Many big international development NGOs, especially Oxfam International, increased their involvement with CAN in response to the prominence of finance and adaptation issues on the climate agenda. This expanded the size of the CAN coalition significantly, adding to its policy depth on these issues.

But this was not the only important change in the world of climate change politics. Preexisting tensions exploded in Bali. There were long-standing disagreements between groups over the appropriate mitigation contributions of developing countries, carbon markets, and tactics. The number of dissatisfied groups reached a critical mass in 2007 and these organizations started holding meetings in a space separate from CAN, discussing their common interests and political positioning. By the end of the Bali meeting, these groups – including Friends of the Earth International, Carbon Trade Watch, Institute for Policy Studies, Jubilee South, Action Aid Asia, FERN, and various smaller Indonesian and Africa groups – had decided to form a new coalition under the name "Climate Justice Now!" The new group coalesced around basic principles regarding exposing "false solutions" to the climate crisis, fighting for climate justice, and promoting reduced resource consumption (Climate Justice Now! 2009).[2]

Climate Justice Now! (CJN) approached the climate change issue from a very different angle than did CAN. These activists began to build an analysis of the climate issue that highlighted the justice dimension and that those most vulnerable to climate change are those who are least responsible for historical emissions. As a CJN press release from 2008 stated:

The historical responsibility for the vast majority of greenhouse gas emissions lies with the industrialised countries of the North. Even

---

[2] See Doherty and Doyle (2013) for more detail on this development from the perspective of Friends of the Earth International.

though the primary responsibility of the North to reduce emissions has been recognised in the Convention, their production and consumption habits continue to threaten the survival of humanity and biodiversity ... Indigenous Peoples, peasant communities, fisherfolk, and especially women in these communities, have been living harmoniously and sustainably with the Earth for millennia. They are not only the most affected by climate change, but also its false solutions, such as agrofuels, mega-dams, genetic modification, tree plantations and carbon offset schemes.

(Climate Justice Now! 2008)

This climate justice perspective highlighted the importance of the divide between northern industrialized states and southern developing states – a divide that CAN was accused of downplaying in order to advance international negotiations.

CJN framed its work to appeal to a broader and less technical audience. For example, CJN material often described its work as "a fight for social, ecological and gender justice." At the same time, the new coalition directly competed with CAN by phrasing its work in terms appropriate for submission to the UNFCCC (e.g., "We ask Annex I countries [developed countries] to agree to ambitious emission reductions in future commitment periods in the Kyoto Protocol that will unlock LCA [Long-Term Cooperative Action] discussions about non Annex I [developing countries'] actions based on the availability of appropriate financing"; Climate Justice Now! 2009).

In addition, CJN framed its diagnosis of the climate crisis in ways that would make linkages to trade, agricultural, and gender issues. The coalition tried to develop a broader systemic critique that distinguished it from the narrow and pragmatic approach of most NGOs. As one participant put it:

It was a strategic mistake of the environmental movement in the past to work on issues separately, rather than to make a systemic critique. But it's hard because we need to come up with something that trade unions, farmers and indigenous peoples can all agree on and that will make these different groups understand the importance of climate change. We have to build bridges between all of these different movements. The environmental movement has been too isolated for too long.

(Interview, CJN 2009)

The climate justice approach implied a different framing of the climate change issue and a different set of strategic priorities. This added to the complexity of the discussion going into the 2009 meeting.

THE COPENHAGEN CLIMATE SUMMIT: 2009

Expectations were high for the Copenhagen Summit. Countries had agreed to make this meeting a deadline, and most were sending heads of state to the negotiations for the first time in years. Moreover, the election of Barack Obama had led many to believe that U.S. participation in a global climate regime was at last a real political possibility. The international media and activists alike had begun gearing up for this meeting by the summer of 2009.

But the mood had significantly soured by November. International climate negotiations have always involved an interplay between domestic and international-level policy. But the gap between the commitments of parties seemed impossibly large. The EU wanted to lead by example in the negotiations: its reduction target of 20 percent in GHG emissions from 1990 levels – with a conditional 30 percent increase in the context of a global agreement – was by far the most ambitious offer on the table. The U.S. position was dramatically less: a 3–4 percent decrease in GHG emissions when calculated from 1990 levels (Pew Center on Global Climate Change 2011). Major developing countries such as China and India refused to accept any kind of binding commitment, frustrating U.S. delegates, for whom this was a key issue.

Civil society activism reached its zenith during this time period. In addition to the two existing coalitions, two new coalitions sprang up in the world of climate organizing. The Global Campaign for Climate Action (GCCA) was intended to be the public face of a publicity campaign that supported CAN's insider policy activities (Interview, GCCA 2009). The coalition was run out of the Oxfam International office and took responsibility for an online petition and the massive family-friendly march mentioned in the Introduction.

The second new coalition sprang from a different source. A group of individuals first met in September 2008 to discuss the possibility of more radical direct action around the Copenhagen Summit. The majority of participants had a background in global justice issues, and they decided to form another coalition, Climate Justice Action (CJA).³ CJA was designed as a loose coalition of groups and organizations working under consensus operating procedures. It was designed to be a vehicle for transnational mobilization and civil disobedience before, during, and after Copenhagen.

The global justice movement has been active around a number of international institutions and has always incorporated environmental actors and concerns (O'Neill and VanDeveer 2005; Smith 2001). But very few global justice organizations actively worked on the issue of climate change prior to 2005. As a result of the efforts of prominent organizations and individuals, many activists within this movement came to perceive climate change as part of their core concerns, and they increasingly refocused their efforts on climate change in anticipation of the Copenhagen Summit, organizing dramatic and confrontational protests such those described in the Introduction.

The timing of this shift made sense. By the mid-2000s, global justice activists were becoming increasingly frustrated with their own perceived inability to impact public discourse. Activists in the UK had a disappointing experience with the 2005 Gleneagles G8 Summit and the government-sponsored "Make Poverty History" campaign. On the Continent, the German alter-global movement went through a similar process of critical self-reflection after the anti-G8 Heiligendamm mobilization in 2007. As one prominent CJA activist put it:

In Heiligendamm we kept talking about neoliberalism and [the leaders] had already moved on. In a lot of ways, neoliberalism was already dead at that point – they were even saying that in the *Financial Times* ... And [the leaders] were saying, "look at all the great stuff we do, we're for the

---

³ This coalition did not adopt the name "Climate Justice Action" until March 2009; for simplicity's sake, I will refer to it as such throughout the book.

environment, we're such good guys." And we didn't have any way
to counter that because we weren't where things were happening. So
we started looking around ... And as much as we were a movement
without a story at that point, there was also a story without a movement:
climate change.

(Interview, CJA 2009)

German activists in the global justice movement, like their counterparts in the UK, increasingly perceived that opportunities for
protest against global financial institutions were limited. They
also saw that the issue of climate change offered new opportunities to advance the movement's cause. For these reasons, the
major international summit in Copenhagen appeared an attractive venue for future mobilization. And they increasingly began to
engage in climate change politics, resulting in what Dana Fisher
(2010) has called the "merging of movements" at COP 15.

These activists had a natural affinity with the CJN coalition
working within the UNFCCC process. These two coalitions frequently collaborated during Copenhagen. This added to the
complexity of civil society organizing, as the field was now split
into those taking a climate justice approach (CJN and CJA) and
those adopting a scientifically oriented approach (CAN and the
GCCA). Chapter 2 documents the internal politics of the
resulting network in greater detail.

These divisions and turbulence were echoed in the official
negotiations. After a chaotic first week of talks, heads of state
arrived in Copenhagen for the high-level portion of the COP on
Thursday evening, December 17, 2009. An "accidental"
recording of their discussions the next morning captured world
leaders negotiating furiously on three main sticking points: emissions reduction targets for developing countries, financing, and
monitoring of national actions (Rapp, Schwägerl, and Traufetter
2010). Despite many behind-the-scenes meetings between world
leaders, ultimately the gulf between parties remained too wide to
develop a comprehensive treaty.

The outcome of their discussion was that there would be no
legally binding agreement in Copenhagen, but that states would
set up an international register to monitor one another's

voluntary pledges. The resulting Copenhagen Accord (2009a) also established a fund for short-term financing for adaptation. After announcing what he termed the "only possible solution," President Obama exited, leaving other world leaders to decide if they would accept or reject the text of the accord.

The U.S. delegation initially proposed that this text be adopted formally by the UNFCCC. After an all-night discussion in the plenary, the majority of states agreed to support the Copenhagen Accord, but the states of Bolivia, Cuba, Nicaragua, Tuvalu, Sudan, and Venezuela objected to the weak nature of the text and the nontransparent manner in which they believed it was brokered. Since the UNFCCC functions by consensus and some of these countries blocked the proceedings, the Copenhagen Accord was not formally adopted and became simply a "noted" document of the convention.

Civil society groups were devastated by the outcome of the negotiations. For many, after years of hard work, the outcome was worse than they could possibly have imagined. Friends of the Earth International called the outcome "a disaster for the world's poorest" (Friends of the Earth International 2009). Greenpeace International declared that "world leaders have failed us" and vowed to continue the fight until it was won (Greenpeace International 2009). Groups focused on communicating to the media their disappointment with and outrage at the outcome. But world leaders beat them to the punch: no one was trying to paint the meeting as a success. EU leader Jose Manuel Barrosso spoke for much of the world when he said, "I will not hide my disappointment ... the document falls far short of our expectations" (quoted in BBC News 2009).

THE COPENHAGEN AFTERMATH: 2010–13

A lot of finger-pointing took place immediately after Copenhagen. Various actors and commentators laid the blame for the failure on the United States, China, the Danish presidency of the COP, or the states that blocked the Copenhagen Accord in the final plenary (Corn 2009; Khor 2009; Lee 2009; Lyans 2009; Meilstrup 2010;

Vidal 2009). Beyond particular states, many commentators began to criticize the institutional setup of the UNFCCC more broadly. Many argued that its universal membership, combined with its consensus-based decision rules, was simply too unwieldy to produce any agreement and that other approaches might be preferable (Barrett 2009; Bell and Blechman 2014; Hansen 2009; Victor 2011). Some actors began eyeing smaller institutions, including the Major Emitters Forum and the G20 (Friedman 2009). It seemed possible that the UNFCCC might fall by the wayside.

In this context, the series of small achievements produced at the 2010 COP in Cancun, including a framework for adaptation and the creation of a Green Climate Fund, were perhaps surprising. These outcomes were achieved by gaveling over the objections of the Bolivian delegation (who insisted on the effort's inadequacy) in order to approve outcomes in these sessions. This redefinition of consensus angered some parties, but it also kept the ball rolling within the UNFCCC, answering the criticisms of others (Friedman 2010). Many saw this meeting as a hopeful sign that cooperation within this institution was still possible, setting the stage for future continued talks.

Subsequent COPs in Durban (2011), Doha (2012), and Warsaw (2013) have continued to make steps within the UNFCCC process. The most significant was the agreement in Durban that parties would develop a new agreement "applicable to all parties" – a departure from the two-track system of the Kyoto Protocol (United Nations Framework Convention on Climate Change 2011a). But disagreements on legal form, scale of ambition, monitoring, adaptation funding, and loss and damage for climate impacts remain pronounced and threaten to derail every negotiation. Some see this as growing pains as the UNFCCC sheds the legacy of the Kyoto Protocol, whereas others see it as a process doomed to codify business as usual under the guise of international cooperation. Either way, talks in the UNFCCC are gaining momentum as leaders prepare for the 2015 meeting in Paris. Delegates have set a new negotiating deadline, and world leaders including UN Secretary-General Ban Ki-moon have already begun to raise expectations for this new global summit on climate change.

CONCLUSION

The time period described in this book captures a crucial period in the long-term development of climate change policy. This was a period of great optimism on the part of many citizens and political leaders who believed that an ambitious successor to the Kyoto Protocol was a real possibility. Expectations for the Copenhagen Summit were exceptionally high, as climate change became a major foreign policy issue with which all world leaders were deeply engaged. The failure of the Copenhagen Summit was a blow to the UNFCCC policy process from which delegates and advocates are still learning lessons.

Copenhagen was a moment when civil society groups were present in force. But these groups were not necessarily cohesive in their approach, complicating our understanding of these actors and their roles in climate politics. Traditionally, the politics of the UNFCCC has been the province of a rarified set of scientifically sophisticated environmental NGOs that pursed fairly unified campaigns. In recent years, climate change has inspired the passions of activists and organizations from a variety of backgrounds, utilizing different strategies. This has increased the number of groups attending, broadened the extent of participation, and diversified the nature of the debate.

We know that there were many new entrants to climate politics in these years, and we know that they introduced new diversity to the organizational population. But how did these groups relate to one another? How did their internal relationships affect the functioning of the civil society network? How did the introduction of new groups challenge the strategies of existing groups? Did all of these changes influence the direction of global climate change politics? The rest of this book takes up these important questions.

2

The Emergence of a Divided Civil
Society Network

Chapter 1 documented how participation in climate change politics dramatically increased in advance of the Copenhagen Summit.
There are many reasons to expect that increased participation
would lead to better performance on the part of civil society
networks. Civil society groups themselves actively court new
members and partners. The UNFCCC routinely encourages participation and emphasizes the contributions that civil society
actors can make to improve climate change policy making (United
Nations Framework Convention on Climate Change 2010). The
basic logic here is simple: with more resources and more expertise,
we should expect civil society to be more effective and, in turn, to
exercise more influence on climate policy.

This chapter tells a different story. I argue that to understand
the implications of civil society participation, we need to understand not only the *number* of groups but also the *relations*
between them. In the climate case, as groups became more
numerous, the divisions between them became deeper. Barbara
Unmussig reflected on this issue for the Green Political Foundation in 2011:

For many years, the belief has survived that we are one global civil
society, which – in a historic mission – will save the world in light of
the universal failure of state policies ... At the same time, the international climate negotiation process highlights how large the conflicts of

interest among civil society actors have now become in terms of geography, positions, and ideologies. There can no longer be any talk of strength through unity, of harmony of positions.

(Unmussig 2011)

The types of divisions that emerged in the climate case are probably not uncommon: other scholars have written about conflict and division within populations of transnational activists (Johnson 1999; Maney 2001; Nelson 2002; Hertel 2006; Bob 2012; Cooley and Ron 2001; Smith 2008; Tarrow 2005b; della Porta and Tarrow 2005). This chapter demonstrates that by using network analysis, we can empirically identify these divisions and map the structure of civil society networks over time.

Network analysis allows us to better describe civil society networks. It also provides a theoretical lens to explain why they evolve in the way they do. In this chapter, I draw on social network theory and organizational ecology to understand how rapid population expansion makes maintaining network connectivity more difficult, and the emergence of a divided network more likely.

Existing literature has demonstrated that advocacy networks can exert an important influence in international politics (e.g. Price 2003), but it is only more recently that it has considered how the internal politics and structure of civil society networks can influence the outcomes they are able to achieve (see Hafner-Burton, Kahler, and Montgomery 2009; Sikkink 2009). This chapter considers two important structural characteristics of networks – size and connectivity – and links them to the ability of networks to perform key tasks. I illustrate the connection between structure and performance by documenting changes in the climate change network's performance over time.

MAPPING CIVIL SOCIETY NETWORKS

Margaret Keck and Kathryn Sikkink famously employed the concept of a network in their pathbreaking book *Activists Beyond Borders*. Keck and Sikkink (1998, 26) describe advocacy networks as internally cohesive actors that share common values, discourse, and strategies. Their book demonstrated that transnational advocacy networks can instigate important changes in international politics. In doing so, the authors catalyzed a debate about the limits of state sovereignty and the importance of transnational actors in a globalized world (see also Risse, Ropp, and Sikkink 1999; Khagram, Riker, and Sikkink 2002). It is testament to this earlier research that later scholars take these networks seriously as influential actors (Price 2003).

Despite the clear connection with the tradition of social network analysis, scholars studying advocacy networks have tended to employ the concept of a "network" without necessarily adopting formal network analysis as a research method (but see Carpenter 2011; Doherty and Doyle 2014; Murdie 2014; von Bulow 2010). Although many social movement scholars conceive of movements as networks (della Porta and Diani 2006; Diani 2003; Heaney and Rojas 2015; Juris 2008; Smith 2008), scholars using formal network analysis and those studying transnational advocacy networks often talk past one another (see Kahler 2009). From the perspective of social network analysis, a network is a structure of relations in which actors are embedded. I adopt this view here and argue that social network analysis can illuminate three important and understudied elements of transnational politics.

First, social network analysis offers a concrete research strategy to make relations among actors visible. Prakash and Gugerty (2010, 300) argue that "the current literature tends to 'black box' the individual components of advocacy networks, obscuring whether these components systematically differ in their strategies or motivations." Social network analysis can help us get inside the black box, revealing the internal connections within transnational advocacy networks. I argue that by disaggregating networks we are better able to characterize the dynamics of transnational organizing. This approach echoes Avant, Finnemore, and Sell's (2010, 3; emphasis in original) hunch that "it is not the type of actor but the *character of relationships* ... that is key to understanding global politics."

Second, using social network analysis allows us to uncover the broader structures that emerge from the patterns of relations among groups. We know that many international networks of advocates are united and consensual – but many others are divided and conflictive, and equally deserving of our attention. As Sarah Stroup argues, "the fragmented and dynamic reality of transnational associational life is equally fascinating" (Stroup 2012, 214). Social network analysis provides leverage to describe networks of a variety of forms, to theorize their evolution over time, and to effectively compare them to one another.

Third, once we allow that networks can take on different structural characteristics, we can explore whether network structure influences how groups of advocates perform key tasks and, ultimately, how effective they are. As Ward, Stovel, and Sacks (2011, 248) also note, "Many network analysts following in Keck and Sikkink's footsteps do not emphasize how variation in network structure shapes the processes under investigation." To take one example, networks are commonly regarded as communicative structures through which resources and information flow. From a structural network perspective, the patterning of those channels should influence the rate and extent of that flow. This directly influences whether actors in the network have access to similar information, discourse, and knowledge about strategies of action.

Scholars have already noted the importance of network structure as a determinant of performance and effectiveness. For example, both Clifford Bob (2005) and Shareen Hertel (2006) study networks that involve ties between local and international NGOs, demonstrating how these networks develop tensions over issue framing and tactics. Charli Carpenter (2011) demonstrates that the internal politics of advocacy networks can privilege key gatekeepers in the network, giving certain organizations an inordinate amount of control over the agenda. Kathryn Sikkink summarizes this growing body of work by arguing that "relatively little precise research has been done about the exact structure of international political networks"; nevertheless, "it is possible that the *nature or structure of the networks themselves* contribute to effectiveness" (Sikkink 2009, 237, emphasis in original).

Building on earlier work that examined coalitions and alliances in transnational politics (Bandy and Smith 2005; Tarrow 2005b), research employing formal network analysis is growing. To cite just a few recent examples, Byrd and Jasny (2010) examine the extent of hierarchy in interorganizational networks around the World Social Forum. Von Bülow's (2010) analysis of the networks of organizations contesting free trade in the Americas examines how and why these networks form. Similarly, Doherty and Doyle (2013) examine the structure of internal relations between national offices of Friends of the Earth (FOE) to show connections among offices in different world regions, and Murdie (2014) examines the internal structure of the international human rights network to show how organizations can benefit from network connections.

This book takes these insights seriously. In this chapter, I first describe the structure of the transnational network of climate organizations. I then link changes in the network structure to changes in the way the network performs. The next section describes this strategy in more detail.

THE NETWORK ANALYSIS TOOLKIT

It is important to first explain a bit of terminology for those not familiar with network analysis. Formally, a network is a finite set of actors connected by a set of ties (Wasserman and Faust 1995, 20). The actors in the network – which in this analysis are civil society organizations – are called "nodes." Nodes vary in the number of ties that they have. Ties themselves can represent any number of direct social relations, for example, communication or friendship between two actors. They can also represent joint affiliations of actors with another type of institution or actor. I consider the relations between civil society groups working for climate protection, which I describe and analyze relying on ties based on co-membership in coalitions and co-sponsorship of collective actions on climate change.

Networks vary in their structural characteristics. While there are many ways to describe network structure, I simplify by

(a)   (b)   (c)

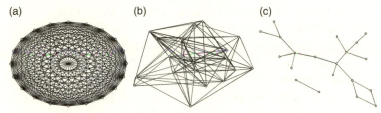

FIGURE 2.1. Sample Networks with Different Levels of Connectivity

emphasizing the importance of two characteristics: size and connectivity. Network size is the number of nodes in the network. In
this instance, the size of the network is how many civil society
groups are involved in climate politics. Network connectivity is a
measure of the extent of connectedness of the nodes in the
network. I interpret "connectivity" broadly in terms of measures
of reachability (Janssen, Bodin, and Anderies 2006), which capture the concept of how easily nodes can contact one another in a
given network structure.[1]

To illustrate the differences between networks with different
structures, I generated three random networks of the same size,
but with different levels of connectivity. Figure 2.1 shows the
differences between the networks. In the network on the far left,
we can see that every node can contact every other node, so the
network is maximally connected. In the network on the far right,
in contrast, two nodes cannot even reach the main component,
and the two sides of the main network component are connected
by only one node. The middle network represents a structural
iteration between these two extremes.

If the networks in Figure 2.1 were mapping relations between
civil society groups, we can understand how their structure
would be politically consequential. The network on the left is
clearly highly cohesive, while the one on the right is more

[1] To do this, I draw on measures of "k-connectivity" in network analysis
(Wasserman and Faust 1995, 266). Given a network, we can measure how
many nodes we would have to remove for the network to become disconnected.
Thus, a highly connected network would have a high k-connectivity score,
whereas a poorly connected one would require only a few nodes to be removed
before it becomes disconnected.

divided. We might expect information to flow more easily in the network on the left than in the network on the right.[2]

The structure of networks can also allocate certain actors to certain roles. One well-known example is the role of a "broker" in a social network. A broker is an actor that links two otherwise unconnected actors (Burt 1992; Gould and Fernandez 1989). Looking at the network on the right of Figure 2.1, the node with two ties in the top middle would be a broker because it joins two otherwise isolated components. The presence or absence of brokers is an important part of what determines overall network connectivity, because if that node were removed, these two components would become unreachable to each other through direct ties.

Based on what we know from Chapter 1, it is clear that the size of the civil society network working on climate change expanded dramatically in advance of the Copenhagen Summit. But without knowing how the structure of ties *between* actors changed, we do not know how the network may have evolved during this period. The next section explores this question.

DIVISIONS IN THE CLIMATE CHANGE NETWORK

Once we allow that networks can have different structures, we are able to consider how they may change over time. The climate case is a good example. As Chapter 1 detailed, as the number of organizations increased, groups formed new coalitions around which to coordinate their actions. Table 2.1 summarizes the development described in the previous chapter.

From 1992 to 2006, the Climate Action Network was the only game in town for transnational climate change organizing. By 2009, three new coalitions – Climate Justice Now!, Climate

---

[2] Some may question whether the figure on the right ought to be considered as two separate networks. Ultimately, the decision of how to define and bound networks remains with the researcher. In my view, it is more useful to consider this as a single network with a low level of connectivity. Doing so allows me to theorize how changes in network structure affect network performance. But by defining the network more narrowly (e.g., by insisting that members of a network must share frames), we could arrive at different interpretations.

TABLE 2.1. *Transnational Climate Change Coalitions, 1992–2009*

	Climate Action Network	Global Campaign for Climate Action	Climate Justice Now!	Climate Justice Action
Acronym	CAN	GCCA	CJN	CJA
Founded	1992	2008	2007	2008
Orientation	Policy	Action	Policy	Action
Framing	Science-based	Science-based	Climate justice	Climate justice
Major Members	Greenpeace, WWF, Oxfam, Friends of the Earth International (pre-2008)	Greenpeace, WWF, Oxfam, Avaaz, 350.org	Friends of the Earth International, La Via Campesina, Indigenous Environmental Network	Climate Camps, global justice movement organizations

Justice Action, and the Global Campaign for Climate Action – had all joined the mix. But what is important for a network analyst are the relations between groups. If these coalitions had many overlapping members, the overall structure of the network may have remained relatively well connected. In other words, to understand the implications of these changes, we need to understand the linkages between the coalitions.

To map the structure of relations among groups, I obtained membership lists for each of the major transnational climate change coalitions present at the UNFCCC in 2006 and 2009.[3]

---

[3] For the Climate Justice Now! coalition, which does not exclusively rely on a formalized membership structure, I pooled the list of its founding members with a list of those that participated in an important network planning meeting in 2009. This procedure is important because I do not want to understate the potential connections between the coalitions. But relying on formal membership lists alone generates very similar results.

(a)   (b)

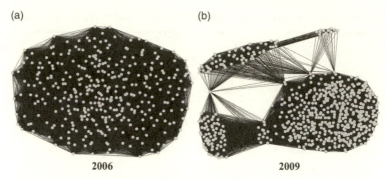

2006   2009

FIGURE 2.2. Network of Organizations Participating in Climate Change Coalitions

I then used these lists of affiliations to visualize the network at two time points. Overlapping membership in coalitions is an important indicator of network structure because shared members can facilitate communication and support cooperation between coalitions (Staggenborg 1986, 384). Figure 2.2 represents the two networks.

In Figure 2.2, circular nodes represent organizations and ties between them mean that they are members of the same coalition. While somewhat stylized, this shows how the climate change network became both bigger and much more divided between 2006 and 2009. According to my data, 365 organizations were members of one major coalition (CAN) in 2006, while 726 distinct organizations were members of one of the four major transnational climate coalitions in 2009. This is a big growth in the size of the network, as Figure 2.2 illustrates.

But there are relatively few connections among the four clusters of organizations in the 2009 network. This makes a lot of sense: coalition membership requires the dedication of lots of time and resources, so most organizations belong to only one coalition. Only thirty-five organizations (5 percent) belonged to two coalitions in the 2009 data, and only three belonged to three coalitions. No organization belonged to all four.

This results in a decrease in connectivity in the overall network between 2006 and 2009. But there were strong connections between two parts of the network: sixteen members joined both the Climate Action Network and the Global Campaign for Climate Action, while Climate Justice Now! and Climate Justice Action had nine members in common. But only seven ties (less than 1 percent) connected CAN-GCCA to CJN-CJA.

Even with few connections, these coalitions might be able to effectively coordinate if they had skilled brokers to connect them. What about the character of brokerage in the network? Closer analysis of the data shows that the organizations that link the two reform-oriented coalitions tend to be big NGOs that have a lot of resources (e.g., Greenpeace, Oxfam, WWF), while those that link the climate justice coalitions tend to be alter-global think tanks (e.g., Institute for Policy Studies, International Forum on Globalization, Focus on the Global South, the Transnational Institute). This shows that big and important brokers join CAN to GCCA and CJN to CJA, but none bridge these two components, making the reform-oriented NGOs and the climate justice movement cohesive subgroups.

These divisions between reform-oriented NGOs and more radical social movements should not be surprising. Sidney Tarrow (2005a) has called these the "two activist solitudes." Jackie Smith (2008b) has documented a similar dynamic within the sphere of the World Social Forum. Donatella della Porta (2007a) has shown that even within the favorable context of the European Union, actors take vastly different paths to trans-nationalization, producing divides that echo what I find in my study. What is unique about the approach I offer here is that I am able to document and describe my network divisions using empirical data on relations between actors.

These data reveal important relational patterns. They are also limited in a number of respects.[4] Co-membership in a coalition

---

[4] There are four main limitations to official coalition membership data. First, not all members in a coalition are active – some are members in name only and not in behavioral terms. Second, these kinds of data underemphasize the importance of the type of actors that make network ties: big, well-resourced organizations are more likely to be important bridges between coalitions than are small, resource-deprived organizations. Third, it ignores ties that are not reflected in formal membership, which are often important conduits of information.

may not be a deep measure of a network tie. For example, when I interviewed one of the major brokers identified in the network analysis, the organizational representative was not even aware that it was part of three separate coalitions. Organizations are also sometimes members of coalitions in name only, or, conversely, they may be active in a coalition but not want their name attached to it.

For example, my interview data and observation of coalition meetings revealed a potentially significant indirect linkage between these two sets of coalitions through the national FOE offices. Although Friends of the Earth International had withdrawn from CAN by 2008, some of its member organizations decided to stay within the CAN coalition. It does seem as though some information could have flowed through the two sides; however, even though FOE could have brokered connections between the two sides, the organization was reluctant to do so. The next section explains why.

EXPLAINING NETWORK DIVISIONS

Social network analysis is useful for describing networks. It can also draw attention to relational dynamics that help explain why networks evolve in the way that they do. As the previous section showed, as the climate network grew in size, it also became less connected and more divided. Drawing on network theory and organizational ecology, I argue that at least two reasons explain why a growing network may have trouble maintaining its connectivity.

First, bigger networks increase the chances of conflict. Scholars of organizational ecology emphasize that growth in the size of a population can lead to increased competition for

Fourth, these kinds of data may ignore ties that exist on the individual level. My research suggests that the first three limitations do not substantially affect the conclusions of my study. Although I do not think that individual overlap is extensive between the two alliances, this study has not gathered comprehensive data at the individual level.

resources (Hannan and Carroll 1992; Hannan and Freeman 1987). Given limited resources – such as members, meeting space, or media access – an organization's population size can grow to the point at which it exceeds the carrying capacity of the system.[5] At this point, organizations will begin competing with one another for limited resources, making cooperation less likely to occur.[6] In this vein, Debra Minkoff's (1994) work shows how population-level effects can have a big influence on organizational foundings and failures, as well as relationships between social movement organizations.

The story of the formation of Climate Justice Now! illustrates this logic. Although, obviously, preexisting ideological tensions existed within CAN, part of the reason for CJN's split from CAN was that the meeting room was physically incapable of holding all of the individuals who wished to participate (Interview, Climate Justice Now! 2010). While dissatisfaction predated Bali, it was not until the number of civil society groups in the population reached a critical mass that the split occurred. And while the increased diversity of the organizational population was undoubtedly beneficial for broadening the debate on climate change, it also led to the creation of additional coalitions to capture these new and diverse interests, fracturing the overall network.

Qualitative evidence also supports the interpretation that the growing size of the network increased conflict. Michele Betsill predicted this development in 2006: "Many observers attribute CAN's influence on international climate change to its ability to coordinate [environmental NGO] activity. However, such coordination is becoming increasingly difficult due at least in part to

---

[5] Organizational ecology suggests that it is difficult to define ex ante exactly what the ideal organizational population size will be. But, following the biological metaphor, at any given time resources such as access to meeting space, negotiators, media, and funding are finite. Increasing the organizational population puts additional demands on these limited resources. The population exceeds the carrying capacity of the system when the demands of the population grow faster than the available resources.

[6] For a similar line of reasoning, see Cooley and Ron (2001).

the growing number of organizations participating in the negotiations" (Betsill 2006, 191).

New groups in the network often believed that they had to
distinguish themselves in the negotiations. They began to compete with older organizations to "take over their political space."
As one explained:

> The big NGOs are totally unable to react to the most important political
> issues of the COP ... We showed them that we really want change; we
> aren't just going to wait behind our stands and give out leaflets and hold
> stupid side events. And I think that should scare them. And it makes us
> reevaluate what kinds of relationships we might want to have with them.
>
> (Interview, Ecologistas en Acción 2009)

This competition stimulated and perpetuated the network
divisions.

Second, network theorists suggest that the size and density of
networks are generally inversely related: an increase in the
number of actors usually means a decrease in the density of ties
in the overall network (Mayhew and Levinger 1976). This is to
be expected, as actors in a growing population cannot dramatically expand the number of their contacts without expending
additional resources on coordination. Thus, most actors can be
expected to maintain approximately the same number of connections, letting the overall density of ties in the network fall as the
size increases.

Previous literature on transnational advocacy networks has
pointed to the importance of their density as a predictor of their
performance (Keck and Sikkink 1998). Density, in network
analysis, can be defined as the proportion of existing ties to
possible ties (Wasserman and Faust 1995, 271). According to
Keck and Sikkink, the denser a network, the better it should
perform. But not only has this prediction not been supported in
empirical network research (Carpenter 2011); also, density and
connectivity should have different implications for network functioning. Recognizing this distinction between density and connectivity helps explain why social capital is sometimes described
as having a "dark side" (Portes and Landolt 1996). Dense social

ties within groups, in combination with limited connectivity to other groups, can breed insularity among members. These cohesive and insular subgroups may limit innovation and facilitate maladaptive or undesirable behavior, such as gang violence, fraternity hazing, xenophobia, or terrorism.

Networks can decrease in density but maintain connectivity if there are strong brokers to connect the different components of the network. Bigger networks will usually need stronger brokers to link the different components and subgroups. For example, Heaney and Rojas (2014) show that "hybrid" organizations that span the boundaries of different movements were critical in the mobilization of the post 9/11 antiwar movement in the United States.

Most network theory has traditionally predicted that brokerage would bring advantages to an organization. Burt (2010, 111) suggests that brokers have "vision advantage," which should allow them access to informational resources from different network components. Marsden (1983) also emphasizes that brokers have a structurally advantageous position from which they can control the flow of resources and, hence, the terms of exchange or interaction.[7] But more recent work highlights that brokerage is hard. Stovel and Shaw (2012) emphasize that brokerage may even have disadvantages, depending on the configuration of the network. Brokers that are biased in their patterns of ties, for example, may lose the trust of one side, as they are perceived as not being neutral. When brokers bridge cohesive groups, they may be perceived as outsiders and viewed with suspicion. Thus, in many contexts, brokerage simply may not be an attractive option.

The experience of FOE clearly illustrates the downsides of brokerage in the climate network. The level of internal solidarity in each side of the climate network made brokerage a difficult task. FOE representatives noted drawbacks to being a broker in this network. As one described it:

---

[7] This parallels Carpenter's (2011) argument that highly central gatekeepers are important in determining which issues are adopted by transnational advocacy networks.

I think this is a strong position because we are able to link two different things that otherwise would be unconnected. We get a lot of info from both sides ... At the same time, it makes our identity more complicated. People feel like we're never 100 percent their allies. We're always the ones that don't quite belong, and we get looked at suspiciously sometimes because of that.

                              (Interview, Friends of the Earth France 2009)

Other interviews also established that acting as a bridge between the two sides of the network created additional challenges for FOE. For example, FOE representatives did not find it profitable to share information between coalitions, as one explained in the following conversation:

JH: [FOE Germany] is in both CAN and CJN, right? So do you ever help share information between the two coalitions?
A: No, we don't do that.
JH: Why is that?
A: We don't really see that the two can mix well. Bringing things from one to the other only creates conflict, and it makes people think that we are representing the opposite side instead of being fully their allies. (Interview, Friends of the Earth Germany 2010)

My qualitative interviews showed that FOE groups recognized that they were in a position for potential brokerage. But they also suggest the reasons why FOE offices did not want to take on the broker role in the context of this competitive and divided network (see also Doherty and Doyle 2013, 189). This lack of brokerage is another reason why the network became divided. These divisions ultimately also had consequences for network performance, as the next section details.

IMPLICATIONS FOR NETWORK PERFORMANCE

Why does it matter that the network became divided? I argue that a wide variety of network functions – including communication, coordination, and collective action – can be related to the structure of relations between actors. Structural characteristics of networks have been underexplored as explanations for network performance (see Sikkink 2009; Ward, Stovel, and Sacks 2011).

My approach allows me to theorize about the importance of network structure, to measure it empirically, and to examine its concrete effects.

Generally speaking, we expect transnational civil society networks to perform two key tasks. First, networks transmit information among civil society actors working within the same issue area (Busby 2010; Carpenter 2011; Florini 2000; Keck and Sikkink 1998; Princen and Finger 1994). Second, they establish and reinforce common identities, tactics, and frames in order to coordinate collective action (Keck and Sikkink 1998; Smith 2008). In this section, I evaluate how changes in the climate network affect its ability to perform these two tasks.

In theory, having more members in a civil society network should – all else being equal – be a good thing. If networks have more money, members, or technical expertise, we should expect that they would be better able to accomplish their core tasks (Keck and Sikkink 1998, 26). Revisiting Olson (1965, 36), Oliver and Marwell (1988) point out that if the costs of collective action do not rise with the number of actors that share them, bigger groups may actually be more likely to organize. According to this logic, expanding network size should improve performance.

But size matters in other ways too. Take, for example, the difference in classroom dynamics between a 12-person seminar and a 300-person lecture. It is relatively easy to build community and trust in the seminar, but much more difficult to do so in the large lecture. It is generally not possible for every individual to interact personally with everyone else once the population reaches a certain size. Thus, most instructors know from experience that the organizational structure of the large lecture will need to be more hierarchical, and that we can expect the character of interaction to be more formal. This same essential dynamic operates in transnational civil society networks, which also change in character as they grow bigger.

Networks also perform differently depending on how well connected they are. Much of the literature on social capital builds on this assumption. Putnam (2000) interprets social capital in associational terms, relating the ability of associations to produce

cross-cutting connections among members of groups to the production of collective goods such as civic engagement and trust.
Social capital is viewed as the product of the social network's
connectivity and is positively related to a network's ability to
facilitate collective action, build social trust, and respond to
external challenges.

But as networks get bigger, they also tend to become less
connected, as previously mentioned. Network theory would
anticipate that as a network grows in numbers, it would also
tend to develop cohesive subgroups, or cliques. When this
happens, social capital tends to develop within, but not necessarily between, cliques. It may also mean that actors in certain
cliques may not be exposed to innovations and may be constrained by maladaptive practices. Such a network becomes
highly dependent on brokers to bridge cliques if it is to maintain
the flow of communication and resources. The functioning of less
connected networks is also more vulnerable to the removal of
nodes. If organizational brokers are for some reason removed
from the network, the network as a whole risks becoming disconnected. With more redundant ties and higher connectivity,
network performance is more robust and less fragile to these
kinds of threats.

This argument is similar to Granovetter's (1973) classic analysis of relations among groups within neighborhoods in Boston.
Granovetter suggests that the inability of the Italian community
in Boston's West End to mobilize may be due to its inability to
develop bridges among isolated social clusters. In this way, a
community that is characterized by a high level of cohesion at
the individual level (i.e., every member belongs to a densely
connected cluster) may also lack connectivity at the macro level
(e.g., the clusters are not connected to one another, producing
overall fragmentation).

These arguments have clear implications for the climate
change network I examine in this book. Over the course of its
history, the climate change network has transitioned from a
small, well-connected network to a large network with a divided
structure. As a result, my theoretical perspective suggests that

the network should be less able to perform its key tasks: facilitating the flow of information among actors and coordinating collective action.

The next section explores the performance of the network to examine these hypotheses. I compare two iterations of the climate change network: the relatively small and cohesive Climate Action Network (1989–2006) and the more divided 2009 climate change network. I draw on qualitative data and secondary sources to link issues of network structure to performance for this analysis.

PERFORMANCE IN A DIVIDED NETWORK

The climate change network has been small and relatively cohesive for most of its history. Early relations between groups in the 1980s were reported to be highly cooperative and based on the idea of complementarities in their roles and advocacy strategies. Climate advocacy was synonymous with CAN from 1989 to 2006. As CAN leaders note in their reflections on this period:

Even in those early days, the NGOs had some degree of cohesion and effective communications ... [CAN] has increased the capacity of the international NGOs to cooperate with one another and has also given CAN more opportunity to affect the [Intergovernmental Panel on Climate Change] and [Intergovernmental Negotiating Committee] processes.

(Rahman and Roncerel 1994, 244–246)

The cooperative relations within the network persisted once the UNFCCC had been established in 1992. In a study of CAN up to 1995, Peter Newell (2000, 127, 153) writes that CAN not only facilitated close coordination among members, but was also able to exercise a moderate amount of influence over the outcome of the UNFCCC negotiations in its early days.

As previously described, the network did experience internal disputes around the time of the 2000 COP. But it remained cohesive. As CAN leader Matthias Duwe wrote in his reflections on CAN's internal functioning during this time, "One could argue that the degree to which cooperation and support have been happening so far is quite an achievement, which stands out in comparison to other networks" (Duwe 2001, 189).

The network was also considered effective during this time. Reflecting on the Kyoto Protocol negotiations themselves, Michele Betsill and Elisabeth Corell (2001, 97) argue that civil society groups were able to coordinate a persuasive message and make political contacts in order to shape the agenda within the UNFCCC. CAN leaders again attributed this success to their integration as a network, stating that "acting as one network with strong North-South links has strengthened the NGOs' voice in international climate negotiations" (Climate Action Network 2001).

To summarize, the post-Kyoto period brought four major changes. First, the population of organizations working on climate change dramatically expanded. Second, conflict in the network increased as a result of the rapid population expansion and diversification. Third, the connectivity of the network declined, as demonstrated by the proliferation of transnational climate change coalitions working around the UNFCCC and the lack of ties between them. And finally, organizational brokers were unwilling to bridge these divides. These four changes resulted in the emergence of a divided network that was less able to perform two crucial tasks: communication and coordinating collective action. The next sections detail these outcomes.

Communication Breakdown

There is a long history of regarding networks as communicative structures for the production, transmission, exchange, and strategic deployment of information (Keck and Sikkink 1998, 3). The structure of relations among groups can influence the ways in which information flows between them, who has access to which information, and the timing of receipt of that information. In a divided network, we would expect information to flow easily within cliques but may see that communication between cliques breaks down.

This is what happened in Copenhagen. Information simply did not flow readily between actors on opposite sides of the network. To document this, I analyzed the flow of emails over official list servs. The fourteen days of the Copenhagen Summit were an intense period of communication among groups – 1,620 emails were sent over the CAN, CJN, and CJA list servs.[8] However, the number of cross-postings – emails that were sent or forwarded to CAN as well as to CJA or CJN – was very small. In total, only thirty-one emails (2 percent) were cross-posted across lists, indicating that the two components were not involved in explicit coordination at the membership level.

Leaders did not report much communication either. Ruth Reitan (2010) argues that the heads of each of these coalitions did collaborate on a few occasions, such as in coordinating official interventions. But this seems to be the exception to the rule. As a leader of CAN International put it when asked about contact with climate justice groups during Copenhagen, "it just wasn't on my radar" (Interview, CAN 2011). CAN meetings are always closed to non-members, so climate justice groups were not able to attend without an explicit invitation.

A number of good reasons can be cited for the lack of communication between groups. One is that there were so many participants that leaders in each coalition were overwhelmed simply communicating with their own members. If communicating within a coalition of 500 groups was hard, dealing with another 200 outside of one's own coalition was nearly impossible. Staff reported that this demand for intracoalition communication was insatiable and directly detracted from their ability to engage in advocacy.

As a result of this lack of communication, different portions of the network had access to very different kinds of information during the Copenhagen Summit. My observation of separate coalition meetings at the time, for example, suggested that

---

[8] During this time period, the author was subscribed to the internal mailing lists of CAN, CJN, and CJA, but not to that of GCCA. See the Methods Appendix for more details.

information about the specific developments in the UNFCCC
policy process and opportunities for influence never reached
some organizations in the population. Some groups were completely unaware that contentious protests inside the venue were
planned. While some groups adopted and actively promoted a
climate justice issue frame, others had quite honestly never heard
the term. Groups simply had different perceptions about what
was going on depending on who they were talking to at the time.

This meant that the total population of civil society
organizations present in Copenhagen never communicated as a
whole. The existence of competing currents within civil society
was picked up in newspaper reports, which often focused on the
in-fighting between organizations rather than their demands (see
for example Zeller and Kroldrup 2009). One of the results of this
was that civil society groups did not develop a common issue
framing or message to present to the news media and to official
delegates, as they had at previous negotiations. This meant that
civil society groups were never fully able to "speak with one
voice" to the international negotiations, which had been a core
strategy in the early days. Chapter 6 further explores the implications of this development.

Coordinating Collective Action

Transnational networks also work to facilitate collective action
among their members (Keck and Sikkink 1998, 25). But when the
structure of a network becomes more divided, it can be hard for
the network to build enough social capital and trust to generate
coordinated action. In turn, such a network may be less able to
coordinate collective responses to external challenges. The two
components of the Copenhagen network were divided on both
the kinds of political relationships they pursued and the tactics
they used. As a result, they frequently worked at cross-purposes –
though this was not necessarily intentional – undermining each
other's strategies of influence.

It was clear in Copenhagen that there was little trust between
the two sides of the network. One example comes from a rare

attempt at coordination: the negotiation between groups over the Global Day of Climate Action, as described in the Introduction. The two sides of the network were planning very different actions for this day. GCCA had planned a huge family-friendly climate walk that would have people converge on the Bella Center and demand an ambitious climate treaty. CJA, on the other hand, had planned decentralized actions and a "radical bloc" that would march separately to demand climate justice, potentially engaging in property damage.

When GCCA leaders found out that a more radical coalition was planning actions for the same day, they became concerned that these groups would spoil their plans, which were the center-piece of their Copenhagen strategy. The GCCA decided to send representatives to the CJA meeting to try to talk them out of their more radical action plans. It did not go well. GCCA representatives were effectively heckled by CJA participants, who shouted: "You're the reason we have to do this!" The lack of trust was palpable to those in the room.

Friends of the Earth was in a difficult position trying to negotiate between these two sides. Eventually, its members became so overwhelmed by their attempt to coordinate these two coalitions that they withdrew from the march and sponsored their own demonstration earlier in the day. The more radical groups did eventually decide to join the march, but formed a bloc that walked at a distance behind the other marchers. Many participants in this part of the march were arrested, while the mainstream marchers were not. This differential treatment by authorities only heightened the tensions between the two sides of the network that did not want to risk being associated with each other, for different reasons.

This lack of trust made it hard to coordinate collective action and strategies, both inside and outside the negotiations. While many reform-oriented NGOs were working tirelessly in the halls of the conference, other groups were organizing confrontational actions outside the meeting space, including an attempt to try to shut down the UNFCCC through direct action. These efforts had unanticipated consequences: as noted in the Introduction,

when outsider groups tried to disrupt the summit, the UNFCCC
Secretariat responded by restricting accreditation for *all* civil
society groups for the final three days of the summit (Fisher
2010).

The failure to coordinate on a tactical level was a particular
blow to those groups that intended to heavily lobby their
delegates in the final hours of Copenhagen. This restriction
almost completely undermined CAN's strategy of last-minute
advocacy with heads of state within the negotiations. Conversely,
without the participation and support of the mainstream environmental groups, those engaging in confrontational actions did
not have sufficient numbers to pull off the dramatic action they
had hoped for. Instead, this action was easily overpowered by the
police, and the radical activists' message did not often make it
into media accounts.

Moreover, the divisions in the network meant that civil society
groups were not able to effectively protest their exclusion. When
the groups were excluded, they did not join forces in protest;
instead they remained divided, even while working within sight
of one another in their new coordinating space outside the venue.
For some groups, this was a strategic decision not to draw media
attention away from the developments of the negotiations themselves; others, however, were interested in contesting their exclusion but could not do so without the support of the broader
network.

Overall, the network divisions meant that groups on either
side tended not to trust each other. As a result, they did not
coordinate their strategies of influence, often working counter-
productively or at cross-purposes. It is important to note that
the use of different tactics within a network is not bad in and of
itself. Many argue that if groups are able to coordinate their
actions, coupling protest and advocacy can be an effective strategy of influence (Haines 1984; Johnson 1999). But the Copenhagen case shows that when networks are divided, these
different strategies can work at cross-purposes, can divide allies,
and can sometimes even undermine the ability of all actors to
participate in the process.

CONCLUSION

This chapter demonstrated that as the number of groups participating in climate change politics increased in advance of the Copenhagen Summit, the structure of relations among civil society groups also became much less cohesive. In particular, divides emerged between longtime NGO participants and those taking a climate justice approach. These groups rarely crossed paths and overwhelmingly failed to coordinate their actions. The extent of these divisions cannot be overstated; as one observer put it after Copenhagen, "we're close to a civil war in the environmental movement" (Komannoff, quoted in Hari 2010).

What were the implications of these changes? I show that divided networks perform differently than their more cohesive cousins. In a divided network, information does not flow as readily and the social capital necessary to coordinate collective action is missing. Divided networks are also more vulnerable and less able to respond to external threats. All of these outcomes can be observed in the case of the climate change network in Copenhagen.

For civil society groups, this suggests an important lesson: growth can have downsides. This lesson is particularly important as the number of organizations engaging in transnational activism continues to grow (Smith and Wiest 2012). While reaching out to new partners and increasing participation can mean more resources and expertise, it can also sow the seeds of division and make overall network performance less effective. The simple logic of "the more the merrier" does not always hold in organizing collective action. This does not mean that there are no benefits to increased size, but it does suggest that these benefits can be potentially offset by decreased cohesion.

For scholars, this chapter demonstrates the utility of studying transnational civil society using social network analysis, which helps us better describe these networks, theorize their evolution, and explain their performance. It also draws our attention to the understudied phenomenon of divided networks and documents how they perform differently than their more cohesive cousins. As my brief examination of Friends of the Earth shows, the structure of networks also has implications for the actors within them. The next chapter demonstrates how and why an organization's position in a network has important implications for its strategic choices.

3

A Network Approach to Collective Action

It was clear by November 2009 that Copenhagen was going to be a very different kind of climate conference. In *The Guardian*'s words:

> Never mind the boring old delegates at next month's climate talks in Copenhagen ... at events and actions around the city, the largest ever gathering of climate activists will take place which aims to create a global network that will take the environment movement forward for the next year and beyond ... It's going to be the sort of fortnight where everywhere you look people are chained to railings with slogans written on their faces.
>
> (Van der Zee 2009a)

Copenhagen was a turning point in terms of the number of organizations that were willing to sponsor contentious collective action. As scholars have noted, before Copenhagen, "few groups ha[d] actively mobilized against the UN" (Smith 2008, 98; but see also Fisher 2004, 179). According to the data I use in this chapter, only 16 percent of organizations used contentious actions more than half of the time in 2008, whereas 58 percent did so in 2009. Sponsoring a contentious action can sour relations with authorities, members, and funders and can incur repressive reactions, making it potentially a costly choice for an organization. So why did so many organizations choose to adopt contentious tactics in this time period? Why did some organizations adopt these tactics while others did not? How did they make these decisions?

The argument I advance here is that organizational decision making is fundamentally relational: it depends on the actions of other organizations working in the same field. Drawing on social network analysis, I show that the ties that an organization has – where it is embedded in the overall network – are consequential for its tactical choices. Specifically, I contend that organizations are more likely to adopt contentious forms of action when their peers have already done so.

This argument differs from most previous theory in that it emphasizes the importance of *relationships* rather than an organization's *attributes* or the *context* in which it works. The influence of relationships can be difficult to detect. The questions asked in this chapter are best answered with quantitative data and statistical methods that allow me to evaluate the strength of my explanation compared to alternative ones. These findings offer a useful complement to the qualitative work presented in Chapters 4 and 5.

For this chapter, I analyze a subset of civil society organizations mobilizing within the European Union. My major hypothesis is that ties with organizations using contentious tactics in the first time period should increase the likelihood that an organization will use contentious tactics in the second period. I test this hypothesis by analyzing a rich longitudinal dataset that combines network data on interorganizational relationships with data on the characteristics of the organizations themselves and the actions they sponsor. My interpretation of these results suggests that if an organization has ties with other organizations already using contentious forms of action in 2008, this increases the likelihood that the organization will itself sponsor a contentious event in 2009, even after controlling for the characteristics of the organization itself and the political context. Chapters 4 and 5 expand on this analysis by showing how these ties form and by what mechanisms relationships influence behavior.

EXISTING WORK ON TACTICAL CHOICES

Explaining tactical choices has been a rich topic for scholars and activists alike. Scholars of social movements, NGOs, and interest groups generally emphasize that organizational tactical choice is explained by a combination of organizational-level factors and external political context (Baumgartner and Leech 1998, 162; McAdam, Tarrow, and Tilly 2001, 17; Prakash and Gugerty 2010). This section briefly reviews these approaches, before I develop my own argument.

A first set of theories argues that different kinds of organizations are likely to make different tactical choices. Two organizational traits are particularly important. First, the kind of resources to which an organization has access – and the source of those resources – should have a large influence on tactical decisions (McCarthy and Zald 1977). Some strategies – lobbying, for example – are expensive. Other strategies, such as protests, require that an organization be able to mobilize individuals to engage in collective action (Schlozman and Tierney 1986). Access to different kinds of resources makes it easier to make certain choices. Moreover, the source of the resources matters: those organizations that are financially dependent on grants from institutions may be less likely to employ contentious tactics that could damage those relationships (Pfeffer and Salancik 1978; see also INCITE! Women of Color Against Violence 2007; Edwards 2008).

The identity of the organization is also important. The adoption of an identity – as a pragmatic, reform-oriented NGO or a radical uncompromising outsider, for example – should influence subsequent tactical choices. Scholars of the framing process suggest that the "symbolic life" of social movement organizations may constrain the ways in which they define problems, solutions, and ultimately the kinds of actions that seem desirable or appropriate (Snow and Benford 1988). Members and funders are drawn to organizations because of their identities or "brands" (Barakso 2010). As a result, organizations need to design collective actions that appeal to constituents' ideological preferences

and preexisting collective identities to avoid alienating their sup-
porters (Brulle 2000; Carmin and Basler 2002; Dalton 1994).

The organizational approach goes a long way to explaining
the differences between groups and their choices. But it is less
suited to explaining why organizations may decide to change
their tactics, especially if their other attributes are unaltered.
Early work proposed a simple stage model – organizations
become less radical over time – but that has not been supported
in empirical research (see Michels 1958, 37; Rucht 1990). More
recent work in population ecology echoes this focus on tactical
stability by suggesting that organizations tend to specialize in
certain tasks or types of action (Polos, Hannan, and Carroll
2002) and that organizations can be punished by both organizational insiders and those outside the organizations when they
violate expectations as to how they will behave (Hannan et al.
2006). As a result, one would expect changes in the population to
come from new entrants or the disappearance of older organizations, rather than through changes in the behavior of existing
organizations (Haveman and Rao 1997; Scott et al. 1999).

A second approach argues that the context in which these
decisions are made matters. The same type of organization may
make different decisions depending on where it operates, when it
is making the decision, and what institution it intends to target.
Characteristics of the political and institutional context in which
an organization is operating – called "political opportunities" –
should have an influence on an organization's strategic choices
(e.g. Meyer and Minkoff 2004; Meyer 2004; Tarrow 2011;
Kitschelt 1986; Tilly 1978). The concept of "political opportunities" can be somewhat amorphous, but it generally captures the
idea of how open institutions are to civil society input and
participation.[1] Three elements of this argument are particularly
important for our case.

---

[1] McAdam's (1999) conception of political opportunities includes four elements:
(1) popular access to the political system; (2) divisions within the elite, (3) the
availability of elite allies; and (4) diminishing state repression. I focus primarily
on variation in the first dimension, following Joachim and Locher (2008).

First, opportunities for collective action vary over the course of institutional decision making (McAdam 1999; Tarrow 1989). In some phases, we should expect a great deal of openness in the process; in others, opportunities will be more restricted. When we see an institution that was once open suddenly become much more restrictive, we should also expect to see an increase in protest (Meyer 1993; Schlozman and Tierney 1986; Eisinger 1973; Tilly 1978). Second, organizations should vary their tactics depending on the institution they are trying to target (Walker, Martin, and McCarthy 2008, 38). When civil society groups want to target institutions that are very open and receptive, they may tend to use more conventional forms of action and reserve their most contentious tactics for those that are less open to their demands. Finally, political process research has also shown that openness can expand and contract as a result of issue-specific opportunities, including issue attention cycles (McCammon et al. 2001). The salience of an issue to the general public – generally measured in terms of media coverage – increases the use of outsider strategies, because individuals become more aware of the need to act (Kollman 1998, 58; Mahoney 2008, 41).

Taking context into account helps us explain why organizations may change their tactics to respond to an evolving environment. But it is still difficult to understand why organizations targeting the same institutions at the same moment may choose such different forms of action. As Baumgartner and Leech (1998) suggest in their review of the interest group literature, both context-specific and organizational-level factors are clearly important. But even when the two factors are considered in combination, there is still a large amount of unexplained variance in most studies that consider tactical choices (Baumgartner and Leech 1998, 165). The next section suggests another approach that helps unravel this puzzle.

THE NETWORK APPROACH

A network approach to collective action differs from the traditional approaches in that it considers organizational decisions to be interdependent. This means that knowing the structure of relationships between organizations can be as important as understanding the properties of organizations themselves or the characteristics of the political system in which they are embedded.

The network approach does not disregard the importance of organizational level and contextual factors. Rather, it conceives of relational processes as supplementing and sometimes intervening between these elements and the mobilization of collective action. From this point of view, it matters not only what kinds of resources are available to actors but also how they are distributed, not only what kind of political opportunities are available but also how actors share information in order to perceive them.[2]

This approach builds on existing research about the importance of relationships, networks, alliances, and coalitions in transnational political organizing (e.g., Diani 1995; Klandermans 1990; Levi and Murphy 2006; Saunders 2007). Mario Diani (2003), for example, has long argued that social networks deserve a central position in our theoretical and empirical work. Doug McAdam (2003) calls for attention to network-based processes as one way to animate overly structural approaches to social movement research. Ann Mische (2003) suggests that the intersection of movements and culture may be an especially fruitful place to explore the importance of relational processes.

Based on my data and existing scholarship, I argue that organizations are embedded in interorganizational networks that influence their choices in three important ways. First, interorganizational relations structure the information to which actors have access. Second, they configure the resources available to actors. Third, they may also serve as channels through which social influence spreads across connected actors. All three of these processes make the harmonization of tactics among connected actors more likely, as organizations become more like

---

[2] Von Bulow's (2010) argument about how groups are "doubly embedded" in social and political structure provides a parallel to my reasoning here.

those with which they share information and resources and are influenced by those to which they are connected.

Information Sharing

Political process theorists have demonstrated that the volume and form of popular contention both correspond to the available political opportunities (e.g., Tilly 1995; Koopmans 1995; Eisinger 1973). But these scholars also recognize that it is not the presence of opportunities alone, but also actors' perceptions of these opportunities, that determines the mobilization of collective action (Ansell 2003; McAdam 1999; Rucht 1989). I argue that the exchange of information about political processes and tactical choices should structure how organizations perceive opportunities and action choices for three reasons.

First, many organizations are not able to directly read political opportunities off the political system itself. The international political process on climate change is highly complex, and the opportunities are not necessarily apparent to the uninitiated. Very few organizations have the capacity to follow this level of policy making on their own; instead, they rely on their contacts with other organizations to get information about possible opportunities for influence.

Second, as Granovetter (1973) demonstrates, an organization's perception of costs and benefits partially depends on what it thinks other organizations are likely to do. For example, an organization may perceive that in a closed political system, it is unlikely to gain benefits and likely to incur high costs (in the form of repression) if it engages in a confrontational protest action on its own. However, if hundreds of other organizations are involved, the organization may perceive that the likelihood of success is greater, and that the costs will be lower. In other words, organizational calculations about the costs and benefits of collective action are interdependent, and organizational decisions should depend on the decisions of other organizations with which they share information.

Finally, networks are important as a channel for learning and the successful diffusion of new practices (Davis and Greve 1997;

Givan, Roberts, and Soule 2010; Ingram 2002; McAdam 1995). Relational ties can structure the kinds of action about which organizations are aware when considering their tactical options. Organizations frequently learn about new forms of action – blockading, occupations, and so on – from other groups with which they are connected (Wang and Soule 2012). Coalition retreats may involve skill-sharing workshops at which organizations explicitly teach one another how to use certain tactics.

For example, a nationally rooted advocacy organization may be interested in working on international climate change politics but have only a vague idea of when the United Nations Framework Convention on Climate Change convenes and what kinds of actions would be influential in such a setting. Interorganizational information exchanges can compensate for the lack of political and strategic knowledge within any given organization and can encourage conformity of behavior among those organizations sharing information.

Resource Pooling

At the organizational level, resource mobilization theorists have demonstrated that collective action is consistently correlated with the greater presence of available organizational resources (e.g., Cress and Snow 1996; Snow, Soule, and Cress 2005). Yet these theorists have also recognized it is the process of converting individually held resources into collective resources that is essential for facilitating their use in collective action (Edwards and McCarthy 2004, 116). I argue that the dynamic of resource pooling can be an important factor in the organizational selection of particular forms of collective action because it can allow organizations to overcome their individual resource limitations when they act with others (Lin 2001).

Transnational collective action is frequently coordinated through interorganizational coalitions (Staggenborg 1986; Tarrow 2005b; Lecy, Mitchell, and Schmitz 2010). Previous scholarship has identified interorganizational coalitions as important conduits through which resources are shared

(Levi and Murphy 2006; Staggenborg 1986). Coalitions can be essential to organizational decision making, for example in facilitating the exchange of resources to make certain types of action possible or less costly (Rucht 1989).

For example, a small organization that does not on its own have the money or staff to produce reports and make the personal contacts necessary to lobby its delegates to the UN may be perfectly capable of engaging in this type of action through a coalition. Similarly, an organization that lacks certain types of resources can engage in actions that require those resources when it acts with partners (e.g., a think tank that does not have a structure to permit individuals to join as members but nevertheless sponsors a protest as part of a coalition). For this reason, the number and type of relationships in which an organization is engaged may be as important for its strategic decision making as its individually held resources, and may encourage conformity with its partners.

Social Influence

Interorganizational networks can also be channels for the spread of social influence, because they alter how organizations learn about possible tactics, perceive their success and appropriateness, and interpret or renegotiate their own identities. Network location determines the number and type of organizations – "alters" – to which an organization is exposed. These alters can provide models for behavior, particularly under conditions of uncertainty.

First, organizations are more likely to imitate tactics that they perceive to be successful (Rogers 1995). But when success is not obvious at the outset, organizations often look to other socially proximate groups to determine what kind of behavior is appropriate (Burt 1982). As a result, interorganizational tactical diffusion via social learning should be more likely when organizations perceive themselves to be similar in some way (Soule 1997, 2004).

Transnational organizing coalitions are in many ways ideal incubators for interorganizational learning and the development of perceptions of similarity between groups. Coalition meetings often involve organizations recounting examples of past successful actions or drawing on historical examples to make the case for the likely success of particular forms of action. Finally, interorganizational meetings often center on organizations coming toward a common ground in terms of their political positions, which may open up each organization to the action style of the others, creating ideal conditions for interorganizational tactical diffusion.

Second, cultural approaches to organizational decision making emphasize that social norms within organizations should make certain types of mobilization more desirable and appropriate than others (Zald 2000). In some versions of this argument, organizational collective identities are conceived of as fixed and exogenous to the mobilization of collective action, driving more radical organizations toward radical forms of collective action (Dalton 1994). But I argue that in most instances, collective identities are defined and redefined through the process of mobilization, making relational dynamics inherent in the cultural approach (Mische 2010). Actors working in transnational political arenas and with different unfamiliar partners may, in fact, be particularly likely to redefine their own identity and, in turn, may reconsider what constitutes appropriate tactics (della Porta 2005; Diani 1995; Taylor and Whittier 1993).

Overall, we should expect interorganizational relational processes to influence tactical choices. Interorganizational relationships structure the information available to actors, configure the resources to which they have access, and spread social influence across closely connected actors. The next section presents descriptive evidence that organizations in my population may be harmonizing their forms of action with those of their peers.

MAPPING THE NETWORK: IS CONTENTION
CONTAGIOUS?

Examining the effect of networks on actors requires that we know what the network looks like, what the attributes of the actors are, how the context is changing over time, and what the behavior of the actor was after exposure to the network. To address these issues, I employ data concerning a subset of the population of civil society actors working on climate change issues in the European Union from 2008 to 2009. I gathered data on their transnational actions and ties from press sources and supplemented these data with organizational documents and information about their attributes from website coding. This extensive data collection process is not discussed in detail here, and I invite the reader to consult the Methods Appendix for more information.

Drawing on this rich data allows me to do a number of things. First, I visualize the network of these organizations. In Figure 3.1, ties (lines) between two organizations indicate that they co-sponsored an event. The lines are thicker if they co-sponsored more than one event. The organizations (circles) are shaded by the percentage of contentious actions they employed in 2008 and 2009, respectively. The ties between organizations are held constant to show the expansion of contention in the organizational population between the two time periods.

The patterns of ties are themselves interesting. As in the international network discussed in Chapter 2, we can see some important divisions and major components. The left side of the network represents the big NGOs that are connected through event sponsorship and belong to the Climate Action Network. Starting from the top left, we see the national offices of the World Wildlife Fund, which are all linked to one another and to their European Policy Office. The bottom left represents the Greenpeace cluster, which has a similar structure in which national offices are connected through the European office. In the middle of the left side, we see that the major NGOs – Greenpeace, World Wildlife Fund, Oxfam, and Friends of the Earth – are closely connected to one another and work together frequently, often through the Climate Action Network.

The right side of the diagram represents the emerging world of climate justice activism. This cluster contains many of the most contentious organizations, such as Klimax, Earth First, the

(a)

(b)

(c)

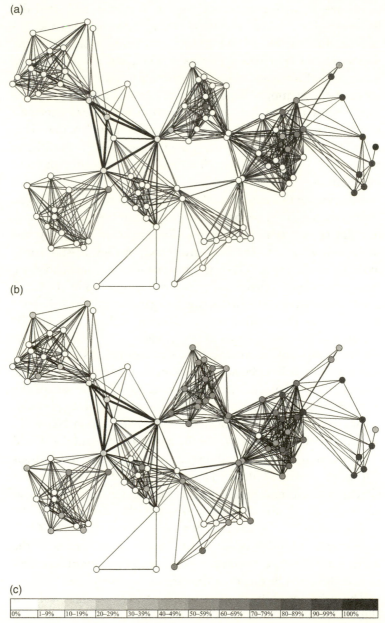

FIGURE 3.1. Interorganizational Network 2008, by Percentage of
Contentious Actions 2008, 2009

Climate Camps, and the Rising Tide Network. The conventional groups in this cluster tend to be small, leftist European think tanks. They are also well connected by dense ties of co-sponsorship.

There are two main bridges in the network. The cluster in the top middle represents the national offices of the Friends of the Earth network. In 2008, Friends of the Earth is linked to both the more conventional NGOs and the climate justice groups, which accurately reflects what is generally known about the internal divisions within this organization. The other major bridge, on the lower right, is made up of critical think tanks and small NGOs working on EU policy. While this cluster is some-what diverse, those closest to the contentious cluster tend to be working on EU policy regarding biofuels and climate change. It is interesting to note that these bridges become less numerous in 2009, making the FOE connection all the more critical.

What is really interesting about this visualization is that it allows us to look at the distribution of tactics within the network. Contention seems to have *spread* between the two years. As Figure 3.1 shows, contention does not spread uniformly across the network, nor does it spread randomly. This figure suggests that contentious behavior is spreading along relational ties. From a few contentious groups located on the periphery in 2008, it has spread to their partners and Friends of the Earth by 2009. This results in the dramatic increase in contention in Copenhagen, but it does not lead to full adoption of the contentious strategy.

This pattern fits with what we know about diffusion in net-works. The literature suggests that the structure of a network and the distribution of innovators within it have important implica-tions for the extent to which new practices are likely to be adopted. Burt (1982) demonstrates, for example, that practices that start at the center of networks spread faster than those that start at the periphery. Moreover, networks need a minimum level of connectivity among cliques – weak ties in addition to strong ones – for innovations to spread between them (Granovetter 1973). Because this network was substantially divided, conten-tion did not spread to all actors.

We can use network measures to examine whether or not organizations are becoming more like their peers over time. Tests for spatial autocorrelation indicate that organizations do indeed seem to be closer to those organizations that use similar forms of action, and that this tendency grows over time.[3] This descriptive evidence suggests that the contentious organizations on the right of the figure have the potential to transmit their contention to others in their cluster. But identifying relational diffusion requires more than descriptive evidence: we must also deal with potential confounders and evaluate alternative explanations for the observed results. The next section describes the research design employed to deal with this challenge.

DETECTING CONTAGION: POTENTIAL CONFOUNDERS

Three potential confounders can make it difficult to distinguish tactical diffusion in social networks from other processes (Fowler et al. 2011). First, network studies are often plagued by homophily bias (McPherson, Lovin, and Cook 2001). Organizations tend to have ties with groups that are similar to themselves (Van Dyke 2003; Clemens and Minkoff 2004). Thus, it is difficult to know if organizations are influenced by one another or whether their common traits are driving similar behavioral outcomes.

I adopt two strategies to deal with the homophily bias in my data. Homophily is less of a problem here than in many network studies because I do not observe ties and behavior simultaneously. Specifically, I use network ties from the previous time period to predict behavior in the second time period, which is particularly necessary when ties are based on event co-sponsorship. In addition, I collected data on a wide variety of organizational traits that I expect to influence the behavior of the organizations in my population. By controlling for these traits

---

[3] Geary's C statistic was 0.38 in 2008 and 0.20 in 2009 (significant at the.01 level in both years) where values smaller than 1 indicate positive autocorrelation.

in my statistical model, I hope to be able to estimate their effects vis-à-vis network ties.

Second, self-selection bias in network studies has to do with the process by which organizations choose their partners. It becomes a concern for this analysis if organizations that select into relationships with contentious organizations are systematically different from those that do not. This may suggest that the results of the statistical analysis may be biased by the fact that assignment to the "treatment" is nonrandom.

My preliminary analysis suggests that there is little difference between organizations that had contentious partners in 2008 and those that did not. Those with ties to contentious groups employed an average of 15 percent contentious actions in 2008; those without ties to contentious organizations employed 11 percent. The difference between the two was not statistically significant in a two-sample t-test, suggesting that tie formation is not patterned by choice of action forms.

But other attributes might also be important. I tackle this issue by using a random intercept model to try to measure the extent to which my data exhibit significant interclass correlations that might suggest unobserved, organization-specific variables not present in the model. Significant interclass correlation would suggest, in this case, a possible unmeasured variable that accounts for selection into contentious relationships and is correlated with the outcome.

Finally, studies of diffusion and behavioral change in networks have to take into account that the actors in the population share a common environment, exposing them to the same exogenous pressures. Two varieties of this problem are present in my data. First, these organizations all have access to the same media, which means that contentious tactics may be diffusing in this population through indirect channels in addition to (or instead of) relational channels. Second, these organizations all share a common institutional environment and are exposed to the same changes in political opportunities. Therefore, their behaviors may change uniformly as a result of this common exposure. I attempt to deal with both of these potential biases by including variables measuring indirect diffusion through media and changes in political opportunities in my final statistical model.

MEASUREMENT AND VARIABLES

For my analysis, I collected data from press sources and documents on 110 organizations active in both 2008 and 2009. These organizations sponsored 165 unique transnational collective actions on climate change in 2009, 35 percent of which were coded as contentious actions.

The dependent variable in this study is the choice of an organization to employ a contentious action. The model predicts the probability that an organization will employ a contentious action and includes actor, network, and event covariates. Many of the actions reported in my data are co-sponsored, yielding 405 unique event-by-actor combinations in 2009, 45 percent of which are contentious. Thus, this analysis weights events unequally: events with more than one sponsor count for one decision on the part of each organization involved. This choice reflects the analytic goals of the study and the fact that co-sponsored events are often bigger and more substantively significant.

The main independent variable is an organization's amount of exposure to contentious organizations in the previous time period: its network embeddedness. I measure this as the number of ties an organization has with contentious organizations in 2008. Contentious organizations are defined here as those that use more than 50 percent contentious actions in their overall action profile (e.g., two contentious actions out of three total actions).[4]

---

[4] Theoretically, I do not consider organizations inherently contentious or conventional and acknowledge that an organization's tactics are a product of choices, not innate character. But for the purpose of this analysis, I define groups that are already using contentious forms of collective action most of the time in 2008 as contentious because of their pattern of choices, not because of their inherent traits. Doing so allows me to emphasize their ability to act as innovators and to spread new tactics in the climate change network.

TABLE 3.1. *Example of Data Structure*

	Contentious Event (Y=1)	Actor A Sponsors	Actor B Sponsors	Actor C Sponsors
Event 1	0	1	1	1
Event 2	1	1	0	0
Event 3	1	1	0	1

TABLE 3.2. *Example of Data Structure, by Actor*

	Percentage of Contentious Actions in 2008	Contentious Organization in 2008 (Y=1)	Number of Ties to Contentious Organizations in 2008
Actor A	0.66	1	0
Actor B	0.00	0	1
Actor C	0.33	0	2

This measurement captures those organizations that were already adopters of the contentious repertoire in 2008.

Table 3.1 offers a hypothetical example of what the data structure might look like. The data have an event-by-actor structure that includes data on the characteristics of events and their sponsors. This example shows three events and three actors. Events 2 and 3 are contentious, whereas Event 1 is not.

I use this event-by-sponsor data to construct my key independent variable, measuring actor embeddedness in the network. For example, Actor B sponsors 0/3 contentious events and thus is not coded as contentious. But Actor B co-sponsors Event 1 with Actor A. Actor A sponsors 2/3 contentious events and is coded as a contentious organization. Thus, Actor B is coded as having one tie with a contentious organization in 2008, despite never having previously employed contentious tactics (Table 3.2).

My hypothesis is that Actors B and C should be more likely to sponsor contentious events in 2009 because they both have ties with Actor A, which is already contentious in 2008. Since Actor

C has two ties to Actor A, it should be even more likely to sponsor contentious events than Actor B. This reflects the "logic of embeddedness" that guides the relational perspective.

I also control for previous behavior by an organization in the final model. For example, I account for the fact that not only do network ties vary, but also Actor B has an action profile that is 0 percent contentious in 2008 and Actor C's profile is 33 percent contentious in 2008, which may indicate a predisposition toward contention.

I introduce variables into the model to account for hypotheses from the political process approach as well. First, I code whether the target of the event was the European Union or the United Nations. In the time period of this study, all of the events that targeted the United Nations took place during the Copenhagen Summit. Following Joachim and Locher (2008, 8), I classify the European Union as more open to civil society participation than the UNFCCC. As a result, we may expect more contention around the Copenhagen Summit than in other time periods.

I also include a variable capturing "indirect exposure" to contentious behavior through popular media. I measure this by the number of reports of contentious actions reported in my press sample in the previous month. This measure is meant to capture the possibility that organizations are imitating strategies that appear successful without direct contact with those using them.

Finally, I include a number of variables capturing organizational traits in order to deal with hypotheses from the organizational literature that help account for possible homophily effects. I include dummy variables for having a 'radical' ideology (those organizations with anticapitalist or antisystemic leanings) and having individual members, as well as measures of the number of full-time staff and the age of the organization. I use number of staff employed by an organization as a proxy for the size of its budget.[5] Finally, I pool institutional records from the European Commission and the European Parliament to determine whether

---

[5] I tried to collect data directly on the size of organizations' budgets but encountered too much missing data to use this variable in the final analysis. The two variables are highly correlated for the cases on which I have data (.87).

an organization received funding from the European Union. The Methods Appendix contains a full codebook and summary of the variables used in this analysis. Additional analyses and robustness checks employing alternative measurements and specifications are provided on my website.

METHODS

To assess my network explanation vis-à-vis other theoretical approaches, I estimated a model predicting the probability of an organization sponsoring a contentious event in 2009, taking into account characteristics of both the event itself and the organization that sponsors it. In my data, I observe multiple responses (events) for the same organization. Therefore, the events observed might not be independent from other events that are sponsored by the same organization. This is a problem because non-independence can cause clustering, and this can cause the usual standard errors to be incorrect (Hosmer and Lemeshow 2000).

I use two methods to correct for this. First, I estimate a logistic regression model with clustering on organizations to generate cluster-robust standard errors (Long and Freese 2006). Second, I use a random intercept model that takes into account the hierarchical nature of the data in estimating both coefficients and the extent of intraclass correlation.[6] My use of a random intercept model also helps control for unobserved variables that are group-specific. Because of a concern that the results may be affected by selection bias, the use of the random intercept model increases my confidence in the estimated coefficients, assuming that these unobserved determinants of selection are time-invariant (Winship and Mare 1992).

A comparison of the estimated coefficients from the logistic regression with clusters and the logistic regression with random

---

[6] In essence, the random intercept model allows the intercept to vary for each cluster while estimating a common slope. Thus, random intercept models are useful for capturing the distinction between effects of covariates that are within-cluster and those that are between-cluster. As there is no a priori reason to prefer either estimation method, I employ and compare the results of both.

TABLE 3.3. *Comparison of Logistic Regression with Organizational Clustering and Logistic Regression with Random Intercepts*

	(1) Logit with Clustering	(2) Logit with Random Intercepts
Number of Ties with Contentious	.311***	.318***
Organizations in 2008	(.105)	(.114)
Political Opportunities		
EU Target	−1.78***	−1.77***
	(.418)	(.431)
UN Target	.934**	.953**
	(.472)	(.451)
Reports of Protest in Previous Month	.001	−.002
	(.035)	(.037)
Number of Contentious Actions in 2008	.112	.117
	(.128)	(.135)
Has Radical Ideology	3.09***	3.12***
	(.986)	(1.14)
Has Individual Members	.155	.154
	(.456)	(.417)
Receives EU Funding	−.283	−.267
	(.427)	(.378)
Number of Full-Time Staff	−.001	−.001
	(.003)	(.003)
Age	.020	.020
	(.016)	(.016)
Constant	−1.30**	−1.30**
	(.555)	(.600)
Sigma_u		.253
		(.559)
Rho		.019
		(.083)

Note: Robust standard errors in parentheses.
*significant at 5 percent;
**significant at 1 percent;
***significant at .1 percent.

intercepts shows that the direction, magnitude, and significance of the effect are consistent (Table 3.3). The lack of strong intracluster correlation means we can be confident that the results are not overly biased by self-selection into the treatment.[7]

RESULTS

My results support the network approach. The analysis suggests that an increase in an organization's number of ties with contentious organizations in 2008 does increase its propensity to sponsor contentious events in 2009. The effect is also substantively meaningful: when other variables are at their mean, if the organization sponsoring the event goes from the minimum (0) to maximum (9) number of ties with contentious organizations in 2008, it is 55 percent more likely to sponsor a contentious event in 2009. Increasing the number of ties by one standard deviation (about 2) increases the probability of sponsoring a contentious event by 17 percent. The number of contentious events an organization sponsored in 2008 is not a statistically significant predictor of behavior in 2009, confirming that organizations changed strategies a great deal during this period.

My results suggest that both the political opportunity and organizational approaches have merit. If an event targets the European Union, for example, it is 41 percent less likely to be contentious than if it targets another institution. If the event targets the United Nations, it is 23 percent more likely to be contentious. In other words, Copenhagen was itself a draw for contentious activism, as we might intuitively expect.

The results also suggest that having a radical ideology is a significant and important predictor of using contentious tactics. When other variables are held at their mean, adopting a radical ideology increases the probability of sponsoring a contentious event by 56

---

[7] The results from the random intercepts model also suggest that the interclass correlation is fairly limited (.019). The likelihood-ratio test that rho is equal to zero suggests we cannot reject the null hypothesis that the between-cluster variance is zero.

percent. This effect is particularly dramatic when organizations have few ties to contentious organizations, but less so when the number of ties with contentious organizations increases. Many organizational characteristics are not significant predictors of contention. Neither age, number of staff, receipt of EU funding, nor the presence of individual members is a significant predictor of contention. Indirect diffusion has virtually no effect, suggesting that most of the diffusion is happening through relational channels.

Since actual organizations have different combinations of these traits, it can be useful to consider a few hypothetical examples based on the model. For example, we can predict the probability of sponsoring a contentious event for a hypothetical organization that was founded in 1985, has a lot of money, receives money from the EU, does not have a radical ideology, and has no ties to radical organizations in 2008. The model suggests that this organization has a 38 percent chance of sponsoring a contentious event during the Copenhagen Summit. But if that organization has two ties to a contentious organization in 2008, the probability jumps to 50 percent. And for an organization with the same characteristics but the maximum number of ties to contentious organizations in 2008, the predicted probability of sponsoring a contentious event in Copenhagen is nearly 90 percent. In other words, changing the characteristics of an organization's personal network would be likely to have a big effect on its choice of tactics.

ILLUSTRATIVE EXAMPLES

Looking at a few actual cases from the dataset should further illustrate the relationship between the variables in the model. My approach highlights that organizations that have similar traits and share a common environment can be embedded in different portions of the network. They can be exposed to dramatically different organizational alters and influences within the same network, resulting in substantially different behavior.

Transport and Environment (T&E) and Gender and Climate Change are both NGOs with nonradical ideologies that combine climate change policy with another substantive issue. Both

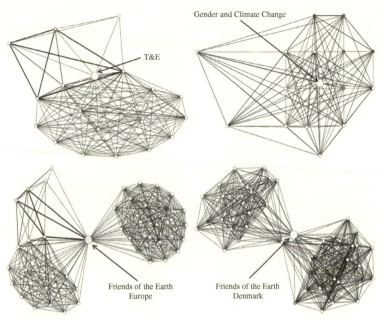

FIGURE 3.2. Egonets for Selected Organizations, 2008

organizations had an action profile in 2008 that consisted of no contentious actions, but with a very different pattern of ties. Figure 3.2 visualizes these egonetworks, representing organizations already employing contention as dark gray nodes. T&E's network of ties with other organizations in 2008 included no contentious organizations; Gender and Climate Change's network included six ties to contentious organizations. Thus, while T&E was exposed primarily to the world of conventional activism, Gender and Climate Change was making contacts in 2008 with a number of contentious organizations that could influence its choice of action forms in 2009.

Similarly, both Friends of the Earth Europe and Friends of the Earth Denmark share an organizational brand and regular ties both to each other and to other FOE offices. FOE Europe used 4 percent contentious actions in 2008, while FOE Denmark used exclusively conventional forms of action when acting transnationally. However, these organizations differed substantially in their ties to other organizations. While Friends of the Earth Europe was embedded in a network that included only conventional organizations, in 2008 Friends of the Earth Denmark was already connected to the emerging world of contentious climate activism.

As Figure 3.2 illustrates, the world of climate change organizing in 2008 looks very different from these various vantage points. Some organizations – such as Gender and Climate Change and FOE Denmark – were already exposed to contentious organizing at this stage. They were engaged in collaborative behavior with contentious organizations and were likely sharing information, resources, and ideas with one another. As a result, Gender and Climate Change sponsored 70 percent contentious actions in 2009 and Friends of the Earth Denmark sponsored 66 percent. In contrast, organizations that lacked exposure did not radicalize in the same way. Friends of the Earth Europe sponsored only 12 percent contentious actions in 2009, while T&E did not choose to sponsor any. This example again suggests how relations may be a crucial factor in determining whether or not organizations adopt contentious forms of action. The next two chapters explore the origin of ties and the nature of their effects in greater detail.

CONCLUSION

The results of my statistical analysis break down the various influences on an organization's choice to sponsor contentious transnational collective action. My analysis suggests the utility of the network approach to collective action. It also suggests that the magnitude of the effect is substantial: small changes in the composition of an organization's network can have a big effect on its behavior. This supports the relational argument about the importance of embeddedness and shows how the diffusion process operates at the organizational level in an actual social network. This approach could be usefully applied to other social movements and contexts to explain how and why we see protest expand in networks.

The network division documented here and in Chapter 2 has important implications for how frames and tactics spread within the network. As network theory would predict, my analysis suggests that organizations have a tendency to match the strategies of their peers. But in the case under study, because of the segmentation of the network structure, there was never any strategic convergence in civil society en masse: the innovations that appeared in one densely connected cluster spread quite quickly but never made it to the population as a whole. So even though some groups were quick to adopt protest strategies, the network never coalesced on this tactic. Similarly, the conventional groups in the population had little contact with those in the opposite cluster, meaning that they had little opportunity to counterbalance the influence of the contentious groups in the population. Chapter 6 considers the political implications of this strategic division.

The network approach I develop has several implications. For organizational theorists, it suggests an interdependent view of organizational decisions. I argue that network ties can be more important than attributes, and that organizations are better understood in relation to one another than on their own. This vantage point also suggests a new research agenda focusing on how organizational characteristics may lead to tie formation or may condition the impact of ties on behavior.

For political process theorists, this approach helps unpack the conditional effect of structure on agents. The theory and findings of this study suggest that political structures do influence the forms of action that groups use when they contest climate change. But the effect of this structure is not uniform, and some organizations systematically seem to ignore political opportunities. In other words, the results suggest that structure is important, but agency is real. I argue that by focusing on network structure, we can better appreciate the channels through which agents can operate, overcome structural incentives and institutional norms, and generate resistance to dominant social and ecological paradigms.

My quantitative findings support the network approach to collective action. But the analysis is limited to a small population of actors working transnationally in Europe; thus, it is difficult to generalize from this analysis. For example, it may be that the European organizations included in this study tend to be more inclined toward contention than those in North America (Rohrschneider and Dalton 2002; Hadden and Tarrow 2007). and have more resources than those in developing countries (Dalton, Recchia, and Rohrschneider 2003). It may be that this was a particularly uncertain time period in which organizations may have been more likely to change strategies. European organizations may be slightly more likely to have international ties than those groups in other regions (Rohrschneider and Dalton 2002, 519), making the relational dynamic more important in this region of the world. These findings will eventually need to be replicated with a broader set of actors and in other time periods.

The next two chapters consider two questions that emerge from this analysis: Why do actors harmonize with their peers? How do they develop these relationships in the first place? I answer these questions by drawing on extensive fieldwork and interviews with civil society organizations from this population. Chapter 4 considers those organizations that employed conventional forms of action. Chapter 5 complements this analysis by looking at those organizations that adopted contentious forms of action.

4

Conventional Climate Advocacy

This chapter deals with the portion of the interorganizational network engaged in conventional climate change advocacy. Individuals working in this sphere were tireless in Copenhagen period. One described the experience of COP 14 in 2008 as follows:

> I've been up since 7 a.m., every day, because I've had to meet with the coordination group in the morning. I do media; I meet with my working group. Then I have to go to the CAN coordination meetings – two of them every day of course. I'm, of course, really here to meet with delegates and discuss our issues. Sometimes it's hard to remember that. Getting intelligence, feeding it back to the working groups, writing statements, sending them to the media. I barely eat – I don't have the time. Last night I was up until 2 a.m. because I was working on an article for [the NGO newspaper]. It's completely exhausting. But I just keep asking myself, if we didn't do it, who would? You know that the business groups are working twice as hard, so we have to be here too.
>
> (Interview, Climate Action Network 2008)

The activities described – lobbying, working with the media, and writing articles – are all well-established routines within the Climate Action Network (CAN). CAN is one of the biggest and most professional transnational advocacy networks in the world and was well established by the start of this study. Despite our interest in transnational advocacy networks, we often know little about the ways in which they form and the internal struggles and compromises that keep them together (but see Bülow 2010). The first part of this chapter examines CAN's internal politics to explain how organizations came to form this coalition, and why it took on the structure and character that it did.

The second part of the chapter explains how embeddedness in the CAN coalition influenced the tactical and framing choices of its member organizations. I show how organizations working within CAN shared information and pooled resources, leading them to adopt similar forms of action. I also suggest that the social influence of important actors working on this side of the network convinced other groups to resist radicalization even when conventional forms of action were less obviously useful.

Chapters 4 and 5 form a pair and complement Chapter 3. My statistical analysis suggested that having ties with a contentious organization increases the probability that an organization will itself employ contentious forms of action. This and the next chapter explain why I observe this relationship in the quantitative data. I particularly focus on why organizations develop ties with other groups and how different patterns of ties influence an organization's choice to employ contentious or conventional forms of collective action.

To answer questions about how organizations make decisions, it was required that I go inside those groups themselves. Chapters 4 and 5 rely extensively on my original qualitative data. This research responds to a long-standing call for more meso-level qualitative fieldwork on collective action (McAdam, McCarthy, and Zald 1988, 729). These data were collected during eighteen months of fieldwork from 2008 to 2009, during which I conducted interviews, observed organizational meetings, and gathered documents from organizations and coalitions active in transnational collective action on climate change.

I reconstruct this period by relying on four main data sources: (1) transcripts from interviews with more than ninety organizational representatives; (2) field notes from roughly 200 hours of participant observation at organizational meetings and actions; (3) internal and public organizational documents, including emails from internal and interorganizational listservs; and (4) existing secondary sources and scholarly accounts. The Methods Appendix describes these sources and research procedures in greater detail for the interested reader.

BUILDING THE CLIMATE ACTION NETWORK

Environmental activists first became interested in transnational coordination on climate issues in the late 1980s, as explained in Chapter 1. CAN was formed to facilitate their interaction in these early years. Most of the individuals involved were already well acquainted from previous international campaigns, including the negotiations over the Montreal Protocol. The expansion of CAN membership involved a social process that scholars have called "scale shift" – the scaling up of activism from the national to the transnational level via processes of brokerage and relational diffusion (McAdam, Tarrow, and Tilly 2001; Yeo 2009; Reitan 2007).

Climate activists were savvy about building their coalition along relational lines. Friends of the Earth, Greenpeace, and the World Wildlife Fund used international campaigns to encourage their national members to engage with CAN. These national groups, in turn, shifted their activism from domestic environmental advocacy to lobbying at the international level. In countries where there were strong domestic environmental movements, major domestic NGOs utilized preexisting contacts to join CAN. New CAN members were required to seek letters of recommendation from current CAN members, underscoring the importance of relational diffusion. As a result, the initial CAN coalition was composed mostly of national chapters of big NGOs and major domestic groups in Europe and North America.

CAN staff began a deliberate effort to expand the geographic coverage of the network in the late 1990s. Staff reached out to environmental groups in underrepresented regions, including Africa, Southeast Asia, and Eastern Europe. Staff commonly put organizations in contact with others working in the same region so that they could share skills and develop contacts in order to ultimately make a successful bid for CAN membership. This brokering connected previously unrelated groups and encouraged them to scale shift to transnational politics, expanding the CAN coalition in turn (Duwe 2001, 182).[1]

The growth in CAN membership was small at first. At the time of the first COP in 1995, CAN had roughly 150 organizational members. Membership stabilized at around 300 organizations throughout the early 2000s. But membership growth took off quickly after that. Whereas there were 365 members of CAN at the 2007 COP in Bali, the coalition had 492 members at the 2009 COP in Copenhagen.[2] Demand to join the coalition was so overwhelming that some CAN regional offices, including CAN Europe, put a freeze on new membership applications until after the Copenhagen meeting. My review of the membership lists shows that most of the growth in CAN membership can be attributed to national environmental NGOs' interest in transnational coordination. Development organizations concerned about the effects of climate change on vulnerable states also formed a large component of the new CAN membership, as documented in Chapter 1 (see also Cabré 2011).

Growth in membership was not the only big change for CAN. Another was that the proportion of civil society groups covered by the coalition was decreasing. For example, in 1995, CAN had more member organizations than the total number of registered nongovernmental observers organizations to the UNFCCC. In 2001, CAN had 328 members relative to 494 registered observers to the UNFCCC; in 2007, it had only 365 members relative to 846 registered observer organizations; and in Copenhagen in 2009, there were 1,297 registered

---

[1] There was a slightly different dynamic in the EU, where many national groups decided to participate more directly in climate change politics after the U.S. proposal to include nuclear energy in the clean development mechanism in the early 2000s. The dynamics of this conference also stimulated the creation of new climate-focused groups, including Rising Tide (Rootes 2012).

[2] CAN membership figures are drawn from internal membership lists provided to the author.

observers, but only 492 members of CAN.[3] These data suggest that more and more actors were opting either to go it alone or to join alternative coalitions in the post-Kyoto period. This chapter describes the CAN approach and its strategies in Copenhagen. The next chapter tackles the alternatives.

THE CAN APPROACH

The Climate Action Network has a distinctive approach to climate change politics. Throughout most of the history of the UNFCCC, CAN has been the central focal point for coordination of environmental NGOs – ENGOs – working within the negotiations. Numerous scholars have documented the successful operation of the CAN coalition in earlier phases of the policy process (Betsill and Corell 2001; Newell 2000; Rahman and Roncerel 1994; Duwe 2001). Central to CAN's advocacy has been the idea that member organizations must "speak with one voice" to influence the international negotiations. Although the exact contents of joint positions are subject to negotiation, three elements have remained consistent in CAN's positioning.

First, CAN targets its advocacy toward the United Nations Framework Convention on Climate Change. While member organizations and regional coalitions frequently work with other targets, the Climate Action Network is focused on securing a good deal within the UN climate process. Second, CAN has traditionally framed climate change as a scientific problem. The coalition's materials try to establish organizations working within CAN as experts in the process by virtue of their engagement with scientific information (Busby 2010). For example, the 2009 joint program of the Climate Action Network for the Copenhagen negotiations stated: "The new science also shows that with any delay in action the costs of mitigation and adaptation increase significantly. Delaying significant actions by even 5–10 years undermines our ability to stay well below 2°C and

---

[3] Official participation numbers are drawn from internal membership lists provided directly to the author and from the UNFCCC (2013).

severely undermines the effectiveness of long-term adaptation action" (Climate Action Network 2009b). The language here frames the climate issue in a scientific manner, addressing its proposals to existing policy tracks within the UNFCCC, and draws on scientific research to justify its policy prescriptions.

Third, the content and the style of CAN materials emphasize scientific urgency as a justification for action on climate change. CAN documents have represented virtually every moment of the negotiations as a "crunch time for the climate" and a "critical moment." This was particularly true in Copenhagen. A CAN newspaper article published on December 17, 2009, titled "If Not Now, Then When?," captures this approach succinctly:

> Since the launch of these negotiations in Bali, a ticking clock has symbolised the race against time to secure a fair, ambitious and binding deal on climate change in Copenhagen. Now the clock is approaching midnight and all eyes are on our political leaders. Can they summon the collective vision needed to secure something positive out of a process that appears to be drifting worryingly towards failure?
>
> (Climate Action Network 2009a)

Painting a negotiation as urgent prioritizes a quick resolution to the problem. Focusing on existing institutions of the UNFCCC suggests that this arena is the appropriate venue for action. And drawing on science to frame the problem of climate change – it is often argued – may detract from views of the problem as one of justice or equity. All of these issues became divisive around the time of Copenhagen.

It is certainly not the case that CAN ignored broader social issues of equity and fairness. But it has tended to address these issues less frequently and in a more technical manner. For example, the CAN joint program from Copenhagen tackled the issue thusly: "Efforts to address climate change must adequately reflect the right to sustainable development and also the principles of historical responsibility and common but differentiated responsibilities and capabilities as enshrined in the Convention" (Climate Action Network 2009b). By using the awkward language of "common but differentiated responsibilities" – which comes directly from the UNFCCC – CAN appeals to an insider constituency of experts. This fits with CAN's historical strategy. But it has also dissatisfied some members, as the next section explains.

DIVISIVE ISSUES WITHIN CAN

Internal disputes became more heated as CAN's membership expanded. One practical consequence of membership growth was the dramatic increase in the sheer amount of coordination required. Staff reported devoting enormous amounts of time to conference calls, emails, and general meetings in 2008 and 2009, simply because the number of people involved had expanded. When the coalition first organized, meetings during COPs would typically consist of 30 to 40 people sitting at a round table; as a CAN staff member noted, "In June 2008 in Bonn, we held our member meetings in a room that was turned into our office space in 2009. So the increase in the number of people in the room was very dramatic" (Interview, CAN International 2010). CAN daily meetings in Copenhagen, by contrast, could often include more than 400 people, sitting in rows in front of a giant projection screen. This expansion, understandably, generated some resentment from longtime members. As one observer put it, "there is a huge new generation of CAN members who have no idea how CAN should function."

Membership expansion was not the only issue: some ideological or strategic tension had always existed between CAN members. Three main areas were divisive in the post-Kyoto period. First, groups varied in their enthusiasm for the use of carbon markets as a policy option for fighting climate change. Many "darker" green groups (such as many Friends of the Earth offices) questioned the environmental integrity of this approach, while "lighter" green groups (such as WWF) were more supportive. Groups faced difficult strategic decisions in light of the negotiations' progress in the late 1990s. CAN's strategy has always been to position itself close to what is politically possible in order to maximize its influence. Thus, it decided to take a position that was mostly supportive of carbon markets, despite much internal disagreement.

Second, the dynamics of the Kyoto and post-Kyoto negotiations deepened the rift between U.S. groups and other groups in CAN. U.S. groups frequently noted that the demands of the international coalition were widely regarded as unrealistic for U.S. policy. For example, while the official CAN position for the Copenhagen meeting was that developed countries should commit to a 40 percent reduction of CO_2 emissions from 1990 levels by 2020, the U.S. administration had only committed to the equivalent of a 4 percent reduction from 1990 levels by 2020.[4] U.S. groups that wanted to lobby their own leaders often took very different positions than the international coalition, which also led to much discontent.

The final cleavage that emerged in the coalition was between groups from developed and developing countries. Tensions between northern and southern CAN members date back to the founding of the network. Northern and southern groups met prior to the start of intergovernmental negotiations to discuss difficult issues related to potential trade-offs between economic development and greenhouse gas emissions. Southern CAN members' positions were similar to those of parties to the G77 at the time, prioritizing southern development and new and additional funding for the environment.

One of the early divisive issues within CAN was that southern NGOs pushed for the centrality of the concept of "equity." The Centre for Science and Environment in New Delhi put forward the core argument in a paper titled "Global Warming in an Unequal World," which presented a critique of the allocation of responsibility for greenhouse gas emissions on a purely national basis, specifically targeting major northern NGOs such as the World Resources Institute for calling for emissions targets that were not sensitive to historical and per capita emissions. CAN pushed for the inclusion of this concept of equity in the UNFCCC

---

[4] These figures are based on calculations done from a 1990 baseline. See analysis from the Pew Center on Global Climate Change (2011).

convention, but the text ultimately did not make it through the early rounds of negotiation (see Betsill 2000).

Some principles of equity did make it into the text of the convention. The most famous is Article 1, which refers to "common but differentiated responsibilities and respective capabilities" and developed countries' responsibility to "take the lead." But the language of this text is intentionally vague and leaves open questions of specific differentiation and sequencing of obligations. Under the Kyoto Protocol, developing countries were not required to make mandatory cuts in their greenhouse gas emissions, while developed countries committed to targets and timetables for emissions reductions.

The political atmosphere shifted as the post-Kyoto negotiations began. Developed countries began to grumble that some developing countries – China for one, but also India – had become major emitters but were not covered under the Kyoto Protocol. And some environmental groups within the United States sided with their government in considering that developing countries had to bear a greater part of the burden in future climate efforts. It became clear that a reconsideration of the differentiation between developed and developing countries would be a major axis of the upcoming negotiations, and that these negotiations could potentially reconsider the issue of binding targets for developing countries.

The political realities of the negotiations re-opened old wounds within CAN. The CAN leadership decided to hold an "Equity Summit" in India in October 2008 to consider the coalition's position on equity issues. The Equity Summit brought 155 participants from forty-eight countries together. As the coordinator stated, "This is an opportunity for civil society organisation members of CAN and non-members (some 20 NGOs) to meet and resolve climate issues leading to tensions between South and North, rich and poor countries, and CAN and other organizations" (Climate Action Network 2008).

CAN members met for several days of intense discussion and debate. Participants identified issues of differentiation, sequencing, and carbon markets as the major areas of tensions that needed resolution. The outcome report of this summit emphasized the importance of the equity issue, stating: "today's world is highly inequitable, and the impacts of climate change are increasing and exacerbating this inequity." The outcome report also recognized the "imperative for survival and sustainable development for the world's poorest and most vulnerable peoples" and noted that developed countries had not fulfilled their commitments to emissions reductions and financial support to developing countries (Climate Action Network 2008). Participants reported that while this summit was important for building trust, it did not break significant new ground on these foundational issues.

There was another important issue on the agenda of the Equity Summit. One of the big (unstated) goals was to convince Friends of the Earth International that it should stay within the CAN coalition. It had been clear since Bali that FOE-I was deeply unsatisfied with the direction that CAN was taking heading into the Copenhagen Summit. FOE-I was a founding member of CAN, but was a darker green organization than many of the other members. The group had been expressing a number of criticisms of mainstream CAN policy, including issues regarding carbon markets, forests, and developing country emissions targets. FOE-I had experienced its own internal struggles in trying to balance the different perspectives and priorities of its northern and southern members (Doherty and Doyle 2013), and these internal disputes resulted in carefully negotiated positions that were hard to re-address.

At this summit, FOE-I leadership expressed reservations about CAN's policy, operation, and strategy. FOE-I Chairwoman Meenakshi Raman explicitly called for the climate movement to work more closely with the global justice movement and to view the negotiations through a lens of climate justice. The organization went back to its membership after the summit for a full vote on whether or not to remain in CAN. The outcome was that FOE-I decided to withdraw. One FOE-I leader reiterated the policy and strategic reasons for leaving CAN in an email on the listserv, mentioning that the organization had decided to dedicate more of its resources to the emerging climate justice movement instead.

CAN leaders were disappointed with the outcome of the FOE-I decision process but, from their perspective, CAN was in a difficult position when it came to recognizing incontrovertible claims for justice and equity, keeping some U.S. groups and 'light green' organizations in the coalition, and remaining politically relevant in the negotiations. As one reflected on that time:

CAN overcomes big divides within the network by balancing concerns from the south with demands of political relevance. This means educating a lot of members in the north about what their southern colleagues want. There is also a growing recognition that what you say at home might be very different from what you say to the international audience. So speaking with one voice remains very important. The idea behind CAN positions is to be as aggressive as possible within the scope of what is politically possible.

(Interview, Climate Action Network International 2011)

Thus, CAN reinforced its strategy of remaining near the mainstream of the political negotiations going into Copenhagen. While this generated tension with groups that had different ambitions, most organizations within CAN considered it an acceptable cost for a growing coalition balancing diverse interests.

CAN IN OPERATION

It has never been an easy task to balance the interests of groups from all over the world. This section details the practices and working procedures of the coalition. The CAN charter calls for the coalition to function according to consensus procedures. CAN uses conference calls and an extensive email list to consult with its membership on the development and adoption of positions, but, as the coalition acknowledges, the positions on which participants are invited to contribute are often "premeditated" by the big member groups. This means that the major international NGOs in CAN – WWF, FOE (pre-2008), Oxfam, and Greenpeace – are extensively consulted before proposals are drafted. Most members acknowledge that the big groups have a de facto veto over CAN positions. If these groups approve of a position, the proposal is then circulated to the entire membership via an email list for an up- or down-vote.

CAN has developed different routines to facilitate decision making when the UNFCCC is in progress. Action or policy proposals are agreed to by a modified consensus procedure. Most of the specifics are discussed in detail by an internal committee system of working groups. Proposals from these working groups are then taken to the daily meeting of all participants, where individuals are asked to vote on them. In practice, consensus at this stage means that no more than 5 percent of members (and none of the big groups) disapprove of the proposal. Most proposals that arrive at the plenary vote tend to pass.

CAN's operating procedures help explain why its members tend to harmonize their positions and strategies. First, when organizations join CAN, they must adopt all of the coalition's existing policies. Second, because of the privileged position given to big groups, many of the positions taken by the coalition are close to those of the more moderate members such as WWF or the larger American NGOs. This internal dynamic results in some darker green CAN members toning down their messaging in order to work within the coalition.

Organizations always have to limit their autonomy to work in coalitions. For many, this is a deliberate strategic trade-off: most groups within CAN believe that by coordinating their activities and speaking with one voice, they increase their chance of influencing the political process (Rahman and Roncerel 1994, 244–6). And securing the participation of larger NGOs – many of which have the expertise and resources to go it alone – requires giving these groups assurances that they will retain some control over the agenda. Understanding the operating procedures and balance between groups within CAN helps explain why we see a fairly moderate policy consensus within the coalition.

Groups within CAN went through complex interorganizational negotiations to arrive at common "asks" for the Copenhagen meeting, including coordinating their demands related to the emissions reductions of developed countries. The resulting position was that developed countries should reduce emissions from 1990 levels by more than 40 percent by 2020. This position was similar to the EU's negotiating offer in Copenhagen and echoed the recommendation of the Intergovernmental Panel on Climate Change's Fourth Assessment Report.

But this position fudges one of the most divisive topics in the network: what proportion of those reductions needs to be made domestically, as opposed to being offset in the carbon market. On this topic, groups widely disagreed. WWF asked for 30 percent to 35 percent to be made domestically, while Greenpeace demanded 75 percent and FOE took the stance that no offsetting was acceptable (Friends of the Earth International 2009; WWF International 2009; Greenpeace International 2009). The CAN compromise position was simply that these offsets should be limited and that unless countries adopted strict targets, there was no need for offsetting at all (Climate Action Network 2009c). Thus, beneath the veneer of consensus, there was often a great deal of disagreement among the major groups in the coalition. This shows how darker green groups – such as Friends of the Earth – would have had to moderate their demands to a fairly large extent to work within CAN.

CAN positions are the result of careful negotiation and often have a large influence on the broader NGO population, even those that are not members of CAN. NGOs that work on climate change will often sign up to, translate, and reuse the materials developed by CAN. It was obvious to a careful eye that many of the NGO lobbying documents used by organizations in Copenhagen were recycled CAN documents translated into another language and with a different name on them. This suggests that what CAN decides has a large influence on what smaller, less well-resourced groups decide to do when acting on climate change.

COORDINATING COLLECTIVE ACTION IN COPENHAGEN

Copenhagen was a key test for CAN's operating procedures. Developing joint positions was a huge challenge for the growing coalition. This section describes how CAN engaged in advocacy and lobbying around this meeting and how it came to support some (limited) collective action at this meeting.

Advocacy and Lobbying

CAN's working procedures encourage members to adopt a professional style of advocacy vis-à-vis the UNFCCC. One the main reasons for this moderation in tactics is that CAN leaders convince member organizations this is the most effective method to use when approaching the UNFCCC. Groups that join CAN get access to listservs on which expert advocates discuss developments in the policy process and suggested responses. New and smaller groups are invited to participate in capacity-building workshops in which groups develop their analyses and discuss the best practices for working with the UNFCCC. These workshops socialize new groups into the working procedures and style of the coalition. Member organizations were invited to a workshop prior to Copenhagen to strategize about the "state of play" regarding the negotiations and where the leverage points for advocacy might be.

During negotiations, the extent of coordination is extensive. An NGO delegate to a COP would likely participate in two to three CAN meetings each day in which political intelligence about the state of negotiations would be exchanged. Working groups report back to the entire membership to keep everyone up to date. Key insights and strategy are also frequently communicated via email lists. Thousands of emails were exchanged during Copenhagen, for example, and the demand for meetings and communication was virtually insatiable.

This political information is put to use in a number of ways. National groups often hold meetings with their delegations to discuss policy options and provide input on national positions. The frequency with which this occurs depends on the openness of the delegation (Bohmelt 2013). Members of working groups within CAN often closely follow the technical details of negotiations. The head of the finance working group, for example, might be asked to speak to the delegate in charge of coordinating this track within the UNFCCC. It is typical for CAN to be asked to give a short speech in the plenary sessions of the negotiating bodies. All of these types of advocacy took place during Copenhagen.

Media outreach is also a big part of the CAN strategy and has three major components. CAN's own daily newspaper, ECO, comments on the state of the negotiations. ECO articles are approved at the daily CAN meeting and often combine humorous commentary, original analysis, and biting criticism of some delegations. The coalition also coordinates a well-attended daily press conference for international media. Speakers and topics for this press conference are approved by the media point person and by the general body in the daily meeting. CAN and its members also work together to sponsor a series of side events that aim at educating members, delegates, and the media about CAN's positions in the talks (Schroeder and Lovell 2012). During Copenhagen, many CAN members considered media outreach to be one of the most important components of civil society participation.

Organizations learn from their peers how to engage in these kinds of activities. CAN holds a weekend strategy session for member organizations prior to every COP. At these sessions, organizations come together to finalize their plans for the meeting and to gain political intelligence from one another. These sessions are also a crucial venue for groups that are new to the process to learn CAN's work routines.[5] For example, the Copenhagen strategy session included one breakout group on how to work within the UNFCCC and another that outlined a typical day in the life of a climate campaigner at the COP.

---

[5] Wang and Soule (2012) find that tactics tend to diffuse from larger to smaller groups. My study of the CAN coalition supports the idea that interorganizational coalitions can also be venues for learning and the diffusion of tactics, and that the dominance of large groups within coalitions means that smaller groups tend to imitate the larger ones.

When all goes according to plan, these different advocacy strategies complement one another and the coalition functions like a well-oiled machine. The highly professional style of advocacy used by CAN may seem surprising to those attached to the radical image of environmental groups. But as Christopher Rootes (2003) documents, this moderation in activism matches what we know about environmental activism in many advanced industrial societies. This professional style is not just apparent to insiders. For example, during a meeting in the UK prior to Copenhagen, Yvo de Boer, then the executive secretary of the UNFCCC, reportedly commented informally to development NGOs that he was surprised at "how bureaucratized NGOs are in the climate negotiations." NGO representatives were well aware of these critiques of their "insider" strategies, but these groups tended to interpret these comments as calls to avoid being "captured by low ambitions of political leaders." They have not necessarily taken them as a comment on their tactics and have resisted calls to radicalize, as subsequent sections show.

Protests and Media Stunts

CAN members have always tried to supplement their extensive lobbying activities with creative and media-friendly protest stunts (Hoffman 2008). These actions might include banner hanging, melting ice sculptures, or marches wearing polar bear costumes. For example, in Kyoto demonstrators organized a "die in" outside the conference venue, lying on the ground as if dead in order to highlight the seriousness of the issues at hand, as well as a basketball game between "greens" and "climate criminals" to draw attention to their positions. CAN itself organizes a short skit every day of the negotiations, called "Fossil of the Day," at which NGO representatives present awards to the country delegations that have done the most to block progress toward climate protection. This theatrical commentary on the state of negotiations draws a large crowd and is frequently covered in national media.

Small protest events and publicity stunts such as these became much more frequent in 2009. One reasons for this was the development of the Global Campaign for Climate Action (GCCA), which was intended to be the public action arm behind the CAN positions. As the organizers explained, "We envision ourselves as the public protest that stands behind the CAN positions. And a big part of our task is just to show that such a movement exists" (Interview, Global Campaign Against Climate Change 2009). Its main organizational sponsors included many of the same groups (Greenpeace, WWF, and Oxfam) that are core to the CAN coalition. For example, the GCCA organized a rapid response team in the spring of 2009 to develop stunts and public awareness actions to be carried out in national capitals across the world. These activities were closely coordinated with CAN in response to international developments. The actions they sponsored included placing advertisements criticizing key governments and holding demonstrations to draw attention to key moments in decision making.

The GCCA served to bridge the energy of youth-oriented Internet activist groups, such as 350.org and Avaaz, and the more traditional environmental NGOs within CAN; 350.org, for example, had organized its own international Day of Climate Action on October 24, 2009, which CNN called "the most widespread day of political action in our planet's history" (350.org 2009). 350.org was a member of CAN but had broader goals of awareness raising and changing public opinion on climate change. Avaaz.org is a much broader organization without a distinct topical focus. In 2009, Avaaz.org committed a good portion of its resources to mobilization around the Copenhagen Summit, using the GCCA as a means to connect its organizing resources to the policy process. Lance Bennett and Alexandra Segerberg (2013) describe this extensive digital mobilization as exemplifying a new type of "connective action" in this sphere.

The GCCA's main activity was sponsorship of a nonviolent, family-friendly climate march during the Copenhagen Summit, as mentioned in the Introduction. These marches have been sponsored since 2005 by a small organization out of London calling itself the Global Campaign Against Climate Change. This march attracted a few thousand people in 2008. Copenhagen continued this tradition, but on a much larger scale. The GCCA mobilized 100,000 people by reaching out to CAN membership and local Danes and Swedes. Its high-profile NGO members brought prominent speakers to Copenhagen and made sure the march was covered in international media. The event was reform-oriented in its messaging and contained in its forms of action. The main portion of the march did not attract police arrests, and the speeches were broadcast to those inside the conference center. The action was not considered threatening by security or the UNFCCC team, unlike other kinds of action, discussed in the next chapter.

RESISTING RADICALIZATION

CAN members overwhelmingly favored conventional forms of action in Copenhagen. But we know that other organizations were making different choices – adopting more contentious forms of action – in the same political context. Why did CAN members not generally adopt contentious forms of action in Copenhagen? The previous section showed how these organizations encouraged one another to use conventional forms of action. This section shows that they also actively resisted processes of radicalization. There are a few reasons for this.

First, groups adopted conventional tactics because they genuinely believed in the power of their own influence. Conventional groups often knowingly decide to accept restrictions on their behavior in exchange for the opportunity for influence (Willetts 1996). They openly acknowledge and weigh the risks of cooptation. One explained the reasoning thus: "Do we get played by them? Of course we do. But at a certain point you have to decide that it's worth it to try and have an influence on the outcome" (Interview, WWF European Policy Office 2009).

This strategic moderation does not mean that the NGOs always support the decisions of institutional actors. Organizations openly acknowledge that figuring out how hard to push them can be a tough balancing act: "We're hard in the sense that they know that we're not just going to roll over when they suggest something dodgy. But they also know that we're not going to propose something off the wall either" (Interview, WWF UK 2009). Organizations often describe their strategic moderation as a trade-off. But they also generally reason that this approach offers the greatest possibility for influence.

Second, institutional rules within the UNFCCC make contention a potentially costly choice. Groups that receive accreditation to attend UNFCCC negotiations have to agree to a code of conduct that limits the scope of their actions. If a member of a group engages in a nonauthorized action, the entire group risks exclusion. Thus, groups that wish to participate in the UNFCCC need to monitor the behavior of their members. During Copenhagen, CAN representatives repeatedly reminded members of the code of conduct to which they had agreed, specifying the clause about "no unauthorized demonstrations" during Copenhagen. CAN groups were made very aware that a decision to engage in unauthorized protest in the conference center could result in the exclusion of other members of their delegation.

Third, CAN leaders acted to contain planned protest actions by other organizations. CAN feared that the status of civil society as a whole might be threatened if any groups appeared irresponsible, and it acted to keep groups from radicalizing. For example, once it became clear that only ninety individuals from civil society representatives would be allowed to be present during the high-level segment of the negotiations (out of the over 13,000 accredited individuals), some individuals and groups within CAN began calling for a mass protest. Others began circulating plans to refuse to leave the venue. Prominent CAN members sent emails urging their colleagues to leave the venue when instructed, warning that any resistance could result in all civil society accreditation being revoked. Youth delegates to the COP, for example, reported that big groups exerted behind-the-scenes pressure to get them to give up their protest plans. In the end, there was no organized resistance to leaving the conference center.

Some CAN members objected to the role of the coalition's leadership in dictating strategy. One individual made an intervention at the CAN meeting the next day in support of developing a broad-based protest to draw attention to NGO exclusion from the venue. A prominent member of the international media even approached CAN to ask if the coalition would consider sponsoring such a protest so that his paper could cover it. But CAN members were not interested in this approach, reasoning that it would only draw attention away from the developments of the negotiations and take the heat off world leaders. In sum, internal dynamics in CAN pushed groups toward moderate tactics and away from more radical protest.

MECHANISMS OF DECISION MAKING

The previous sections examined how the CAN coalition operates in practice. These operating procedures help explain why organizations working in this sphere tended to harmonize their frames, positions, and tactics in Copenhagen. But how do the individual groups working within CAN make these decisions? By what calculus do they decide to adopt one form of action or another? This section employs qualitative data to answer these questions.

I draw on more than ninety interviews with civil society representatives (see the Methods Appendix). My coding of these interviews identifies three important themes in their responses. The interviews reveal how their tactical decisions are driven by the relational mechanisms of information sharing, resource information pooling, and peer influence, corroborating the results from the quantitative analysis in Chapter 3. They also reveal two other important processes. Organizations frequently mentioned that their staff engage in rational evaluation of political opportunities to choose tactics, but the perception of these opportunities often seems limited by organizations' desire to appear professional to external audiences. This section summarizes these data.

Relational Mechanisms

Organizations working in the conventional sphere were clearly influenced by relational dynamics in their decision making.

Chapter 3 highlighted three mechanisms: information sharing, resource pooling, and social influence. Evidence of all three of these mechanisms is found in my interview data.

First, information exchange is a core part of the CAN coalition and contributes to the opportunities which organizations know about. Groups' abilities to evaluate political opportunities are limited by the information that they receive about the political system. The UNFCCC is an incredibly complex and acronym-laden institution, and organizations usually do not have the capacity to follow its negotiations on their own. By joining CAN, they have access to a huge amount of information and analysis of the negotiations and the leverage points at which they can apply pressure.

Information sharing also influences the tactics which organizations know how to employ. Conventional groups teach one another how to engage in lobbying. As the previous section discussed, CAN holds many workshops and meetings to develop this approach. Many small groups report that without CAN emails and listserv discussions, they would not understand the "possibilities for influence in the political process" (Interview, Polish Green Network 2009).

Second, conventional organizations often report pooling their resources to overcome lack of funding or staff. Many organizations cannot afford the staff or office space they need to adequately follow the international policy process. Building coalitions with other groups enables them to engage in forms of action that might not otherwise be possible. Groups that have a particular technical expertise, for example, may not have the resources to target the policy process independently, but this kind of group can work with others with more lobbying experience to coordinate actions (Interview, Wetlands International 2009).

Third, organizations also exercise social influence to persuade one another of the utility or desirability of using certain tactics. Organizations in CAN convince one another of the utility of their conventional advocacy approach. For example, the big NGOs in CAN seem to have a particular influence on the kinds of demands which groups make, as well as the types of actions in which they engage in the international sphere. As one participant pointed out, CAN has a large influence on the kinds of strategies which organizations choose to use: "It seems like in CAN, a lot of the large groups set the tune, and we all tend to follow that. But when we work at home, we can't always sell that, so we might do different things" (Interview, Greenpeace Germany 2010).

The structure of decision making within the coalition allows the big groups to veto any strategic initiative. One anonymous participant noted that this can be highly consequential: "Some NGOs look to CAN for positions and opinions. A lack of ambition within CAN can then have negative influence on the NGO community." This influence extends to tactics as well: as this chapter has shown, CAN leaders exerted a great amount of influence to keep other organizations from radicalizing tactically, even when political opportunities were rapidly closing in Copenhagen. Influence seemed to flow fairly easily between these groups because they had worked together for so long. This helps to explain why we see extensive and persistent use of conventional tactics in this portion of the network.

Rational Evaluation

One of the reasons why we might see tactics vary in response to political opportunities is that organizations may be systematically reading the political system and altering their tactics to maximize the probability of achieving their desired ends (e.g. Marks and McAdam 1999; Tarrow 2011). Many organizations described this kind of rational procedure.

For example, campaigner training materials across Greenpeace, WWF, and FOE encourage staff to identify political opportunities and alter tactics to fit the situation. FOE staff employ a "SWOT" analysis technique – identifying strengths, weaknesses, opportunities, and threats – for the achievement of FOE's aims. Within Greenpeace, this technique is called "power analysis" and is typically taught to new campaigners during organizational training. As one campaigner described it:

We do a power analysis to see what kind of pressure the politicians are susceptible to. Are they susceptible to mobilization? Are they scared of Greenpeace? Can we use the media? Is it better to work through other organizations? We consider questions like this when we decide which tactics are best.

(Interview, Greenpeace Nordic 2010)

The interviews suggest that most environmental NGOs are trained to recognize the opportunities available in a given political environment. Most also suggest that these organizations are theoretically open to altering their tactics to make the achievement of their aims more likely. Overall, groups operating in the conventional sphere often report this procedure of rational evaluation as an important determinant of their tactical choices.

Professionalization

In addition to relational mechanisms, my interview data suggest that perception of the opportunities available to groups is strongly influenced by their desire to appear professional and responsible. This pressure often results from the need to maintain strong relationships with government actors and to secure funding. Scholars have previously documented how professional organizations may need to adopt different forms of action. McCarthy and Zald (1973, 26) argue that professional social movement organizations can "diffus[e] the radical possibilities of dissent ... by applying large amounts of resources ... in ameliorative directions." Staggenborg (1988) argues that the professionalization and formalization of organizations in the pro-choice movement led to its adoption of more institutionalized tactics, because activists were replaced by professionals who wanted to sustain the organization over the long term to protect their careers. Rootes (2012, 52) argues that environmental NGOs simply are not inclined toward radicalism, and "the modal repertoire of institutionalized environmentalism in England was conventional even during the peak decade of environmental protest."

Similar dynamics seem to be operating in the climate change movement. Smaller groups often mentioned that they "follow the money" when choosing campaigns and tactics. As one puts it, this constitutes a form of opportunity:

> We try to identify and act on strategic points. This means working with the opportunities we are provided. [JH: What kind of opportunities are you talking about?] Well, that essentially means we respond to subjects coming from the media and government agenda. Our actions are also largely subject to funding opportunities – what kind of project we can get money for.
>
> (Interview, RAC France 2009)

My interviews suggest that groups try to be seen as professionals and not as activists in the transnational sphere. As an interviewee from Greenpeace EU puts it:

> We don't want to be seen as a bunch of environmental Nazis who like to hang ourselves from things. We want to be seen as professional, responsible people who understand what is politically possible and are experts in our field.
>
> (Interview, Greenpeace EU Unit 2007)

Respondents frequently reported that this commitment to being professional, and this may also help explain the lack of contention in this sphere, as well as the disconnect between the closing down of political opportunities in Copenhagen and the refusal of environmental NGOs to adopt protest tactics.

Overall, the interview data explain some of the correlations I noted in Chapter 3. The measures of political opportunities are important because many organizations rationally evaluate opportunities and vary their tactics accordingly, but the scope of actions may be limited to conventional forms because of professionalization. Relational mechanisms – including information sharing, resource pooling, and social influence – help explain why organizations tend to harmonize their actions with their peers and resist radicalization even when conventional action is less obviously useful. The next chapter expands on this analysis by examining those organizations that did choose to adopt contentious forms of action.

CONCLUSION

The buildup to the Copenhagen Summit was a turbulent time. As one anonymous participant explained to me in 2008, she did not hold high hopes for Copenhagen:

I think the problem is that for those of us working on this now, we weren't around in the 60s and 70s. We don't know what it feels like to win big victories. And I'm fatigued – honestly, I just don't know if I can keep doing this. Every time we get close to something, the NGOs decide they'd rather fight with each other than to push for big change ... And it's going to happen again in Copenhagen, I just know it. It's going to be a circus, and I'm dreading it.

Most of these predictions proved completely right. An explosion of new groups working on the issue area used highly contentious tactics, challenging conventional groups that wanted to use their well-established professionalized advocacy routines. The longtime participants were not only irritated by the newcomers; they were also fearful that the use of radical tactics would result in security restrictions for all participants. Many of the big groups within CAN worked hard to rein in their members and persuade them not to radicalize their tactics in the final days of Copenhagen. My examination of organizational decision making in this chapter suggests that relational processes such as these had an important influence on the ultimate tactical decisions of many groups.

NGOs are not opposed to protest. CAN members such as Greenpeace, Oxfam, and the WWF were, of course, the main organizers behind the massive Global Day of Climate Action. But this chapter should demonstrate that satisfying the different demands of organizations within CAN while remaining politically relevant for the climate negotiations has been a difficult balancing act. Thus, it should not be surprising that the contentious challenge in Copenhagen does not come from the world of CAN: It originates in a separate sphere, as the next chapter documents.

5

Climate Justice Activism

It was clear by November that Copenhagen was going to attract a different kind of activism than previous meetings. The head of the Police Intelligence Service in Copenhagen made a public statement claiming that "violent extremists will try to abuse and get a free ride on the peaceful activist involvement in the climate debate" (van der Zee 2009b). This fear of violence led to preemptive police action. One participant described a raid on activist sleeping quarters:

Last night at about 2:30 a.m. we were all sleeping [in the warehouse] and the [expletive] cops came and woke us all up. They locked us in, and then they raided our supply room. I guess we should have seen it coming – they just came in and raided us. [JH: What did they take?] Like, the riot shields we had been making, some stuff they said could be used to help us get over the fence or in violent activities. They were harassing us too – they handcuffed some people and were telling us that we didn't have a permit to be there. But they [expletive] know that we do, they were just trying to scare us. A lot of people were really frightened and alarmed. And it makes me wonder what we can expect when we go out in the streets on Wednesday.

(Interview, Climate Justice Action 2009)

As the quote illustrates, contentious organizations operate in a different world than conventional groups. Individuals participating in contentious groups spent most of their time during

Copenhagen planning protest strategies, making banners and props, attending the alternative climate forum, speaking to the press, and developing contacts with other activists. Not only does the repertoire of contentious collective action employed by these groups differ dramatically, but they are also engaged in a highly confrontational relationship with political authorities that gives their activism a very different character.

This chapter explores similar questions to those discussed in Chapter 4: Where do interorganizational networks come from? What influence do they have on individual organizations working within them? As in the previous chapter, I draw on primarily qualitative interview data and document analysis. Here, I argue that much of the structure of the contentious portion of the 2008 network reflects the regularized inter-actions of organizations participating in two new organizing coalitions: Climate Justice Now! (CJN) and Climate Justice Action (CJA). When these two coalitions appeared on the scene of climate change organizing, they brought new actors to the issue area of climate change and, at the same time, disrupted the pattern of ties of organizations previously engaged in it. In particular, the membership overlap and even-tual alliance between CJN and CJA led to the creation of an important and tactically contentious climate justice challenge in Copenhagen. This had an important influence on the organ-izations embedded in this portion of the network, as this chapter shows.

THE ORIGINS OF CLIMATE JUSTICE ORGANIZING

Chapter 1 documented how many of the critical currents running through climate politics began to re-emerge in the mid-2000s. While the environmental movement has engaged with issues of environmental justice since the 1980s, this strand of activism was beginning to take a more focused shape in climate politics by 2005. But the impetus for forming a new coalition to chal-lenge the Climate Action Network came at the Bali meeting in 2007.

During Bali, a group of individuals began to meet regularly –
and separately from CAN – to discuss a justice-oriented perspective
on climate change. Many of these individuals represented groups
that either were not CAN members or believed their issues were
being excluded from the CAN agenda. These individuals gradually
coalesced around basic principles regarding exposing "false solutions" to the climate crisis (such as carbon markets and geoengi-
neering), fighting for climate justice, and promoting reduced
resource consumption. At the end of this meeting, these groups –
including Friends of the Earth International, Carbon Trade Watch,
Institute for Policy Studies, Jubilee South, Action Aid Asia, and
various smaller Indonesian and African groups – decided to form a
new coalition under the name "Climate Justice Now!"

There was some animosity between CJN and CAN at the
outset – for example, CJN started publishing a newsletter titled
Alter ECO, which was a clear jab at CAN's *ECO* newsletter –
but eventually the groups moved beyond this overtly oppositional phase. While CAN and CJN shared few members, there
was a general sense that their work was on some level broadly
complementary. As one participant explained:

> What CAN does and what CJN does are totally different, but ultimately
> kind of compatible. CAN is all about getting a deal within the UN
> process ... but CJN is really a lot broader than that – it's about creating
> social and political change, about reducing consumption, and about
> system change ... and those two things can work together, in theory
> at least.
>
> (Interview, CJN 2009)

CJN had a much less formal structure than CAN. At first, there
was no formal membership process and the coalition's largest
resource was its extensive email list. Big organizational members
such as Friends of the Earth rarely contributed strategic or financial resources to the coalition for fear of dominating the democratic process. Participants reported that in the early days, it felt
as though the coalition was more "virtual" than actual.

Organizers in CJN decided to become more formalized and to
seek out grant money in advance of Copenhagen. They received
enough money from funders to hire someone to deal with media

and to support a limited number of participants from the global south attending the COP (Byrd 2010). The UNFCCC formally recognized CJN as another coordinating body within the ENGO community in time for Copenhagen. This meant that CJN's status was equal to CAN's in terms of securing meeting space, plenary passes, and speaking time (Reitan 2010). Membership in CJN continued to grow as the coalition became more formalized and attracted more attention.

Parallel to the growth of CJN, global justice movement groups were also developing an interest in climate change politics. The global justice movement has always had an environmental component but had not often focused on climate change prior to 2007. The approaches of CJN and this movement had some natural affinities – the global justice movement is often defined based on its use of collective action to further justice promotion goals among people living all over the world (della Porta 2007b, 6). Three preexisting environmental currents within the global justice movement aided in the transition. First, eco-anarchists associated with organizations such as Earth First! or Rising Tide had long bridged the two spheres. Second, German radical left organizations had been interested in mobilizing on climate change since the 2007 G8 Summit in Heiligendamm. Third, the "climate camp" movement had exploded across Europe and the world after the success of the eco-village at the 2005 Gleneagles G8 Summit. As one climate camper put it: "Some people see Climate Camp as the environmental end of the anti-globalization movement, or the anti-globalization end of the environmental movement" (Interview, Camp for Climate Action UK 2009). These strands did not necessarily merge easily (Wahlstrom, Wennerhag, and Rootes 2013), but all were present within the critical sphere of climate activism.

The adoption of climate issues was far from inevitable, despite these affinities and overlaps. Activists undertook significant work to bring about this transition. Scholars argue that movements can spill over from one to another when activists begin to perceive similarities and promote intermovement diffusion (Meyer and Whittier 1994). My research suggests that there was a lot of spillover from the global justice to the climate justice movement in the years 2007–9 as many global justice movement organizations began to consider climate change part of their core concerns (see also Pleyers 2010; Hadden 2014).

This spillover occurred for three reasons. First, starting in 2007, activists in Germany and the UK began to conceptually link issues such as global finance, debt, food scarcity, and militarism to climate change. They perceived that this approach offered them opportunities not presented by discussing neoliberalism alone, as explained in Chapter 1. They established climate change as a symptom of a broader systemic problem. They purposely departed from the technical language associated with environmental advocacy groups and tried to reach out to broader constituencies. For example, prior to Copenhagen, activists printed and distributed pamphlets entitled "Why Climate Change is Not an Environmental Issue." The introduction stated: "This pamphlet looks at climate change from the angles of capitalism, militarism, nuclear energy, gender, migration, labour & class, and food production. Climate change is not just an environmental issue. It is but one symptom of a system ravaging our planet and destroying our communities" (Unsigned Movement Document 2009).

Second, these groups intentionally adopted frames of injustice as a way to broaden mobilization.[1] This was a strategic decision, as one activist explained:

Obviously we want to make the movement as broad as possible. And it's kind of inspiring to see how much and how many movements can fit under this umbrella of climate justice now. So it has the urgency of direct action, it has the justice aspect where you can fit quite a lot of different approaches under this umbrella, and it's about climate but it's about more than climate. I mean, everybody knows that climate justice is also social justice. And it's really comprising quite a lot of different aspects.

(Interview, Climate Justice Caravan 2009)

---

[1] Previous research has shown that the use of injustice frames can be a successful way to broaden mobilization (Cable and Shriver 1995; Capek 1993; Gamson 1992, 112).

Others whom I interviewed echoed this assessment. Many activists explicitly mention broad frames as one of the keys to movement success:

And also [summit protests] are a kind of an umbrella ... In order to unite a movement you need something that is catching all the movements like "another world is possible" or "ya basta!" So you share the rejection, but there are many yeses. And you don't have this if you just have campaigns on single issues. And this is one strength that you get from these kinds of protests – it always worked really well for us to do it this way. [JH: So do you think that climate justice is such an umbrella?] Exactly. It's just that.

(Interview, Peoples' Global Action 2009)

Third, climate justice activists deliberately linked the mobilizations in Copenhagen to previous global justice movement events in order to broaden their appeal. They particularly drew on the historical precedent of the Seattle WTO protests, which were all the more important because the Copenhagen Summit was originally scheduled to open on November 30, 2009 – the tenth anniversary of the Seattle WTO shutdown. As prominent global justice movement thinker Naomi Klein wrote prior to the Copenhagen Summit:

There is certainly a Seattle quality to the Copenhagen mobilization: the huge range of groups that will be there; the diverse tactics that will be on display; and the developing-country governments ready to bring activist demands into the summit ... If Seattle was the coming out party, this should be the coming of age party ... The Seattle activists' coming of age in Copenhagen will be very disobedient.

(Klein 2009)

Thus, climate justice activists developed a new frame that bridged the radical environmental community and the global justice movement in an attempt to make Copenhagen "the new Seattle." They mobilized new types of actors and brought them together with others with whom they had not previously worked. This is consequential for several reasons, as the next section explains.

WHO JOINS THE CLIMATE JUSTICE MOVEMENT?

The world of climate justice activism was originally very small. At first, CJN was composed of only a few organizations, many with small staffs. Only a handful of global justice activists in Denmark, Germany, and the UK were deeply interested in climate issues. The community of eco-anarchists on the Continent could not have numbered more than a few thousand.

These individuals began to come into contact with each other in late 2007 and early 2008. The UK Climate Camps were an early beacon in the organizing effort, and many international activists traveled to these events. A group of young Danish activists was particularly enterprising in building connections. They were motivated to initiate a mobilization at COP 15 for a number of reasons. They had had a dispute with their government about a squatted youth center in Copenhagen; some of these activists believed that the government had mistreated them in this struggle and wanted to embarrass Danish leaders on the international stage. But more importantly, many of these activists were interested in honoring the anniversary of the Seattle WTO shutdown with their own radical mobilization, and sought out international colleagues to make this mobilization as large as possible.[2]

These individuals traveled around Europe to the various climate camps and organizational meetings in the summer of 2008 to try to convince people and organizations to participate in an international meeting on the Copenhagen Summit in September 2008. Invitations to this meeting were distributed widely across activist listservs and websites. In addition, the meeting was to take place two days before the European Social Forum (ESF) across the border in Malmö, Sweden. The ESF itself was expected to attract 80,000 participants from a wide variety of leftist backgrounds, so the timing of the event was aimed at attracting the broadest possible spectrum of groups.

The first meeting of the coalition that would become Climate Justice Action was organized by a group of individuals

---

[2] As with most social movements, there was a debate about the correct strategy. Some Danes took the opposite view, trying to discourage participants from the UK from coming to Copenhagen because of concern about infrastructure and emissions from travel.

from the climate camps, from the radical left, and from eco-anarchist groups. As one observer quipped, it was "a small group of European professional activists – all the usual suspects really." A number of representatives from Climate Justice Now! were also invited to speak about climate justice politics and to give background about the UNFCCC meeting in Copenhagen.

Who were these organizations? My informal count of the stated backgrounds of participants suggested that one-half were environmental activists and the other half had a background in anti-summit organizing. Drawing on the European data from Chapter 3, I note that two organizational characteristics distinguished climate justice groups. First, organizations of the same generation did seem to flock together. Most organizations in CAN had been founded in the 1980s; in contrast, most of those in the climate justice coalitions had been founded in the late 1990s. Second, affiliation with the global justice movement was also much stronger in the climate justice coalitions. Half of those organizations in CJN or CJA had a background in the global justice movement, in comparison with 6 percent of CAN members; 79 percent of CAN members were classified as environmental organizations, in comparison with 33 percent of members in the climate justice coalitions. These data are clearly limited to a subsample of the organizational population, but they do provide evidence of some general differences between the two sides of the network.

Initial alliances did not, however, seem to be patterned by action forms. CJN and CJA members employed contentious actions an average of 20 percent of the time in 2008, whereas CAN members used contentious actions 12 percent of the time on average. Although this does suggest that CJN and CJA had slightly more of a predisposition toward contention from the outset, the difference is not statistically significant in two-sample t-tests. This evidence, along with my observations of these coalitions' discussions, suggests that the tactical preferences within the climate justice movement were quite diverse.

THE CLIMATE JUSTICE APPROACH

The climate justice movement differed from the mainstream environmental movement in a number of ways. I emphasize three particularly important intellectual currents: (1) a prioritization of the politics, and not the science, of climate change; (2) a skeptical take on international institutions and a focus on decentralized solutions; and (3) a clear opposition to the use of carbon markets. This section explains these elements in more detail.

One of the influential organizing documents of the climate justice movement explicitly outlines the movement's relationship with science-based discourse. The movement critiqued mainstream environmental groups for framing the issue as a narrow scientific one without highlighting the broader social, political, and economic factors that contribute to the problem. As the document states, this kind of issue framing has defined a limited set of possible solutions:

In spite of its obviously political nature, the issue of climate change is often perceived as a question of science rather than politics. This in turn leads to a situation in which the problem of climate change is exclusively or predominantly framed as a problem that has to be dealt with globally ... through the techniques of scientific and economic management rather than through social and political transformations.

(Brand et al. 2009, 11)

The movement called for broader transformations in response to the climate crisis. It also promoted the use of more decentralized and community-based solutions, drawing on long-standing principles in the global justice movement. The commitment to this approach can be seen in both principle and practice. Climate justice groups established their own social forum in Copenhagen – the Klimaforum – to discuss climate issues in a more "horizontal" space. The "People's Declaration" that emerged from this forum emphasized the importance of decentralization by stating:

This requires a restoration of the democratic sovereignty of our local communities and of their role as a basic social, political, and economic unit. Local and democratic ownership of, control over, and access to natural resources will be the basis for meaningful and sustainable development of communities and simultaneously for reducing greenhouse gas emissions.

(Klimaforum 2009)

The People's Declaration did call on the UN process to produce a binding treaty but also expressed skepticism that this would be possible because of corporate interests, a lack of democracy, and low levels of ambition in the institution. This reflects a schism in the movement between those who believed that the international institutions governing climate change were illegitimate and could never produce a good treaty and those who believed that this was unlikely but theoretically still possible.

Finally, climate justice groups strongly opposed the use of carbon markets as a policy mechanism for fighting climate change. This rejection of carbon trading led to further opposition to the negotiations being conducted within the UNFCCC, as Chapter 1 explained.

The climate justice approach presented a sharp critique of contemporary climate change politics and differed substantially from the approach of conventional advocacy groups. The three positions just described combined to imply a different framing of the climate issue, as well as a new set of tactics and strategies (see also Tokar 2010; Bond 2012). At the same time, its agenda for action was purposely open-ended and broad, as the next section details.

CLIMATE JUSTICE IN OPERATION

The climate justice movement was organized differently than a traditional NGO coalition. CJA adopted many of the operating procedures associated with the global justice movement. For example, the coalition functioned according to procedures of consensus decision making. Proposed meeting agendas were circulated in advance via email, giving individuals time to reflect and contribute. At the face-to-face meetings, designated facilitators raised these agenda items and asked for feedback. During discussions, individuals used hand signals to communicate agreement or disagreement with other people's opinions. Facilitators tested the group for consensus when they believed agreement had been reached; if an individual wanted to block the decision at this stage, the group would return to the discussion. The process repeated itself until agreement had been reached (or until it was decided not to make a decision). This process was quite time intensive in practice. Most CJA meetings lasted several days, and decisions were often not reached on the most divisive topics.

Consensus procedures meant that participants in CJA had to come to full agreement on every joint statement or action proposal. This had important consequences: consensus decision making procedures were a vehicle for harmonization of tactics and frames among participating organizations. This dynamic becomes particularly clear when we consider how CJA approached the task of writing its Call to Action, which needed to summarize the purpose of the movement and attract others to participate. Because this document had to reflect the ideological diversity of the initial participants, the text went through a number of iterations and was subject to agreement by consensus. Figure 5.1 shows a draft version of this call on the left, along with the final version on the right.

An organizing group that consisted mainly of individuals who wanted to engage in direct action prepared the first version of the text, but consensus was only reached by modifying the text along a number of dimensions. Three axes of change are worthy of particular emphasis:

- *Targets*: The original text contained only references to corporate action targets and the inadequacy of "so-called leaders" to solve the problem. The final version of the text scratches both of these elements, retains the language of "acting on the root causes of climate change," but adds a section on targeting "the key agents responsible." The final text bridges the gap between constituencies by being vague about the targets of any eventual action.

Towards climate action in Copenhagen 2009	A Call to Climate Action:
We stand at a crossroads in history. The facts are undeniable. Global climate change, caused by human activities, is happening. We all know that, world over, we're facing a manifold and deepening crisis: of the climate, energy, food, livelihoods, and of political and human rights. Scientific, environmental, social ~~and civil society~~ movements from all over the world are ~~calling for~~ action ~~against climate change~~:	We stand at a crossroads. The facts are clear. Global climate change, caused by human activities, is happening, threatening the lives and livelihoods of billions of people and the existence of millions of species. Social movements, environmental groups, and scientists from all over the world are calling for urgent and radical action on climate change.
~~Massive consumption of fossil fuel~~ is one of the ~~major~~ causes of global warming, a problem that threatens the lives of hundreds of millions of people around the world. ~~Instead of leading the way, governments are prioritizing economic growth and corporate interests while ignoring the speeding train of climate change hurtling towards the abyss. The corporate exploitation of the planet's resources cannot be allowed to continue any longer. We have precious little time to react to this threat. We need action NOW to stop climate change, and if the so-called 'leaders' won't lead the way, we must.~~	On the 30th of November, 2009 the governments of the world will come to Copenhagen for the fifteenth UN Climate Conference (COP-15). This will be the biggest summit on climate change ever to have taken place. Yet, previous meetings have produced nothing more than business as usual.
On the 30th November 2009, world leaders will come to Copenhagen for the UN Climate Conference (COP15). This will be the ~~most important summit~~ on climate change ever to have taken place, and ~~it will determine how the countries of the world are going to respond to the climate threat. The decisions taken there will define the future for all the people of the world.~~ The previous meetings give no indication that this meeting will produce anything more than empty rhetoric and a green washed blueprint for business-as-usual.	There are alternatives to the current course that is emphasizing false solutions such as market-based approaches and agrofuels. If we put humanity before profit and solidarity above competition we can live amazing lives without destroying our planet. We need to leave fossil fuels in the ground. Instead we must invest in community-controlled renewable energy. We must stop over-production for over-consumption. All should have equal access to the global commons through community control and sovereignty over energy, forests, land and water. And of course we must acknowledge the historical responsibility of the global elite and rich Global North for causing this crisis. Equity between North and South is essential.
There is an alternative to the current course and ~~it's not some far off dream~~. If we put ~~reason~~ before profit, we can live amazing lives without destroying our planet. But this will not happen by itself. We have to take direct action, both against the root causes of climate change and to help create a new, just and joyous world in the shell of the old. And so, we call on all ~~responsible~~ people ~~of the planet to take direct action the~~ root causes of climate change during the COP15 summit ~~in Copenhagen 2009.~~	Climate change is already impacting people, particularly women, indigenous and forest-dependent peoples, small farmers, marginalized communities and impoverished neighborhoods who are also calling for action on climate- and social justice. This call was taken up by activists and organizations from 21 countries that came together in Copenhagen over the weekend of 13-14 September, 2008 to begin discussions for a mobilization in Copenhagen during the UN's 2009 climate conference.
The exact plans for our mobilization are not yet finalized. We have time to collectively decide what our best course of action may be. We encourage everyone to start mobilizing in your own countries. It is time to take the power back ~~from the leaders not responsible enough to hold it~~. The power is in our hands!	The 30th of November, 2009 is also the tenth anniversary of the World Trade Organization (WTO) shutdown in Seattle, which shows the power of globally coordinated social movements.
Please circulate, translate and distribute this call widely.	We call on all peoples around the planet to mobilize and take action against the root causes of climate change and the key agents responsible both in Copenhagen and around the world. This mobilization begins now, until the COP-15 summit, and beyond. The mobilizations in Copenhagen and around the world are still in the planning stages. We have time to collectively decide what these mobilizations will look like, and to begin to visualize what our future can be. Get involved!
	We encourage everyone to start mobilizing today in your own neighborhoods and communities. It is time to take the power back. The power is in our hands. Hope is not just a feeling, it is also about taking action.
	To get involved in this ongoing and open process, sign up to this email list: climateaction@klimax2009.org.
	Please circulate, translate and distribute this call widely.

FIGURE 5.1. Draft and Final Version of the Call to Action Issued by Climate Justice Action, September 2008

- *Tactics*: The proposed version of the text suggests that the coalition will sponsor "direct action," but in the final version the term is changed to simply "action." In fact, the final text explicitly mentions that the plans for mobilization are not set and invites groups to participate with their own ideas. This change is also the result of compromise among diverse groups present at the first meeting.

- *Outreach*: The final version of the text tries to reach out to a broader constituency by referencing affected peoples (women, indigenous people, poor people, and farmers). It also drops the term "civil society," because it was thought that this phrase had different connotations in different places. Finally, it adds a reference to the Seattle WTO anniversary, in an attempt to reach out to global justice movement groups.

In summary, after consensus had been reached, the text of the CJA Call to Action became less of an autonomous, direct action–oriented document and transformed into something much broader as a result of group discussion. The point of discussing this example is to emphasize that participation in CJA was initially an agreement in principle to work together, rather than an agreement on specific ideological positions or tactics. Despite the strong preferences of some within the group, neither its ideology nor its action proposals were preset, and both were subject to continuing renegotiation and consensus. Organizations came to cooperate in CJA without necessarily knowing what the final outcome of the mobilization would be. This meant that within the group there was room for a great deal of compromise and influence in the ongoing consensus procedure.

As the modifications to the text also reveal, CJA was concerned from the beginning with questions of how to build the biggest mobilization possible. In general, most of the groups that got involved with the coalition had been targets of outreach by earlier members. Having a vague call helped broaden the potential appeal, but it also made recruitment difficult in some ways. Early organizations had to join the coalition without necessarily knowing what the ultimate action proposal would look like. As one CJA participant complained, "it's pretty hard to build a movement before we know what it's about."

One main venue for recruiting potential participants and organizational sponsors was the European Social Forum in 2008. Although CJA representatives also held a meeting at the World Social Forum in Belém, Brazil in 2009, the scope of the mobilization for Copenhagen was mostly European. CJA's purpose at the Belém meeting was primarily to get input from southern groups, but in general it was not expecting much participation in joint actions in Copenhagen.

CJA particularly targeted groups associated with the CJN coalition. This was natural because some of the original members of CJA were also active within CJN. However, few CJN members were based in Europe, so this effort was important to CJA mostly for symbolic reasons. In particular, CJA was interested in gaining the support of La Via Campesina and the Indigenous Environmental Network, as it was believed that without the support of these groups, actions taken in support of these affected communities would lack legitimacy. This became particularly important once CJA began to discuss the specifics of collective action in Copenhagen.

COORDINATING COLLECTION ACTION: 2008–9

The tactics of the CJA coalition were not decided at the time of its formation, as discussion of the Call to Action illustrated. Organizations worked through a consensus procedure to design a compromise action called "Reclaim Power." This section describes this process.

Toward Tactical Consensus

The conveners of the first CJA meeting clearly intended that the group would organize a classic summit protest. This is not surprising, because the summit protest is perhaps the most visible performance in the repertoire of the global justice movement (e.g. Bennett 2004; della Porta 2007b; Wood 2007). As one early and influential mobilizing document put it:

Where do the strengths of the radical global movements lie both in comparison to our enemies and to our more moderate allies? Answer: in the organisation of large-scale, disruptive summit mobilisations. It is precisely in summit mobilisations that we have developed something that could be called "best practice," where we have before achieved a substantial political effect ... Forget Kyoto – Shut down Copenhagen 2009!

(Müller 2008)

Many of the founders of CJA supported this type of action at the outset of the meetings. But because of the diversity of participants, shutting down the summit was by far the most controversial topic of discussion within the CJA coalition.

This diversity was clear from an exercise facilitators organized at the first meeting: people were asked to engage in discussions with their neighbors about the actions they would like to use to fight climate change, and then to physically arrange themselves along a continuum from most radical to least radical forms of action. At one end of the room, some organizations wanted to use a mass march that would appeal to leaders in the UN to act on climate change and would complement inside lobbying. A proposal in the middle of the room called for groups to hold tribunals for climate criminals outside the venue. At the far end of the room, it was clear that many organizations were committed to a direct action–style shutdown of the conference. No decision was made on this issue during the first meeting because of a lack of consensus.

The next important CJA meeting took place at COP 14 in Poznan, Poland, and changed the balance of positions. Because the meeting was held during a COP, more people came to CJA from NGO backgrounds, and especially from CJN. The Poznan groups were concerned about shutting down the UNFCCC because they believed that the institution could still come up with valid solutions. The groups present at the meeting floated a number of ideas on the CJA listserv about possible "inside–outside" actions that would link mass action outside the conference to strengthening the position of progressive delegations inside. As one anonymous participant put it: "The action has to be strong enough to show what we need – it can't just be a classic demonstration. At the same time, this isn't just a direct action movement, and we need to use our diversity." This topic was hotly debated at meetings and on the listserv, reactivating the original tensions within CJA about the extent to which the coalition would be more radical or more reformist.

The March 2009 meeting of CJA was designated as the crucial meeting for designing the action strategy of the coalition. In advance of the meeting, the facilitators invited various organizations to write up and submit their proposals for an action strategy. These were included in the Handbook for the March Meeting (Climate Justice Action 2009), and participants were asked to come prepared to discuss the proposals and make decisions for their group.[3]

The proposals on the table were quite diverse. The German COP 15 network and the UK Climate Camp proposed the "shut it down" strategy, which was a classic summit action. The Danish groups preferred a "shut them in" or "take it over" strategy. A few international NGOs proposed a mass march and demonstration to call on UN leaders as an inside–outside action. A number of NGOs in CJN suggested an "Ecological Debt Tribunal" outside the conference venue. Groups representing a more eco-anarchist position supported a strategy of targeting lobbyists and problematic delegates to prevent them from entering the venue. All these proposals had strong support from different organizational backers.

The ultimate compromise was perhaps unexpected. One anonymous participant had suggested on the listserv that activists employ a combination strategy of forcing their way into the venue, while some of those inside came out to meet them. This proposal gained support surprisingly quickly, despite a lack of strong organizational sponsors or clarity about the content, because it seemed to be a way of halting the tactical debates that plagued the group. As one participant put it:

At the March CJA meeting, there was consensus that we would organize one central action, so the discussion then became what should we do? The Danes were very attached to the shut in idea. But at the strategic level, such an action involved an appeal to the UN to do something. And that's not what we wanted at all ... Not to mention that at the tactical

---

[3] Two other issues were proposed before this meeting. Some groups associated with CJN insisted that the type of action did not matter as much as the date (it had to be in the second week once heads of state arrived). A German autonomous group proposed that the coalition had to function so that groups could not criticize or disassociate themselves from other groups using confrontational tactics (a common operating procedure in the global justice movement). Both proposals were adopted by consensus at the March meeting.

level, it was never going to work: how are you going to shut people in when you have to stay on the streets of Copenhagen for two or three days in the winter? It just wasn't going to happen. So the next idea was the shut out, which is kind of the classic summit action. But Via Campesina didn't want that, with a bunch of northern activists storming the summit, so we agreed to take it off the table. On the list there was a guy from Geneva who had proposed a kind of inside–outside action, and at the meeting we called this the "meet at the fence" idea. It was still a bit fuzzy, but that was the general idea. And it just sort of took off from there.

(Interview, Climate Justice Action 2010)

By early March, members of CJA had already begun to compromise on the kind of action they would sponsor in Copenhagen. And in this spirit, the idea of the ultimate action – called Reclaim Power – started to take hold in CJA.

Designing Reclaim Power

Reclaim Power was designed as a compromise strategy on the part of the various groups present in CJA. The official action concept for Reclaim Power involved four components: (1) a disruptive outside action; (2) a disruptive inside action; (3) a walkout from the conference center; and (4) a People's Assembly in the area of the conference center.

The disruptive outside action was the biggest component. The concept for the outside disruption was a combination of the German "five fingers" tactic used in Heiligendamm, the UK Climate Camp tactic of converging blocs, and the Danish push-ing tactic.[4] Participants organized in blocs would use different routes and means of travel to converge at the fence of the confer-ence center at the same time. Once they reached the conference center, they would form a mass that would try to push past the police to enter the area inside the fence. Simultaneously,

---

[4] The converging blocs tactic involves multiple autonomous groups that take different routes to arrive at the same site at the same time. The five fingers tactic is similar but involves multiple moving blocs that engage in blockades at different locations. Finally, the pushing tactic simply involves activists forming solid blocs and pushing against the police until they give ground.

participants inside the conference center would cause disruption and stage a walkout from the venue. The two groups would meet outside the conference center and stage a People's Assembly to discuss their own solutions to the climate crisis.

The action itself was a significant innovation in the summit protest repertoire for several reasons. While utilizing well-known tactics associated with the "Seattle model" of protests, such as jail solidarity, protest puppetry, affinity groups, and (limited) blockading (Wood 2007), activists decided against a shutdown approach in Copenhagen, as this would have alienated some influential groups within the coalition. Instead, climate justice activists designed an action that would highlight their own solutions to the problem while delegitimizing the official international process. In addition, this action made explicit linkages between radical social movements, critical NGOs, and progressive country delegations in the negotiations.

It was clear by June that there was tension within CJA because the action was not autonomous enough for some groups. While agreeing to participate in Reclaim Power, these groups also started to proliferate their own more autonomous action plans. These included "Hit the Production," whereby groups would target corporations in Copenhagen Harbor, and "Our Climate, Not Your Business!," which would target corporate delegates to the COP process. A small group did break off to form another (much smaller) organization, calling itself Never Trust a Cop (NTAC), in June 2009.

Once the outline of Reclaim Power was set, CJA started to call on groups to go back to their regions to mobilize and organize similar actions. These actions became much more frequent in the summer and fall of 2009, as groups took these ideas back to their own cities and began to practice them at home. CJA used its extensive membership overlap with CJN to gain support for this action from its close ally: many CJN members signed on as co-sponsors of the action while also engaging in advocacy during Copenhagen.

Some moderate groups expressed discomfort about the design of the central CJA action. Friends of the Earth International decided to pull out, having ultimately come to believe it would be unable to control the direction of decision making within CJA. The fundamental sticking point between FOE and more radical groups was the issue of nonviolence, which FOE strongly supported but some CJA members believed they could not guarantee. A participant characterized the break in these strong terms:

FOE can't be involved in CJA, because of the big question: where will it all end? There is no question that the mainstream of CJA is nonviolent, but who knows what will happen when they get on the streets. Diversity of tactics[5] is a [expletive] British idea. The anarchists love it, and they love using it because that means no one can tell them not to do what they want to do ... The whole rhetoric is to not water down what others do. But as FOE Sweden, we did want to water it down. I don't mind saying that. And we don't support the closing of discussion on it either ... We needed them to be strong on nonviolence and against property damage.

(Interview, Friends of the Earth Sweden 2009)

Because FOE had strong preexisting positions regarding nonviolence, most leaders felt the organization could not participate in Reclaim Power. Representatives also mentioned that FOE does work within the UNFCCC process, and if the organization were to sponsor this kind of action it would lead to serious risk of expulsion.

This meant that CJA ultimately lost groups on both sides of the political spectrum. As one participant summarized:

At the CJA meeting in October, FOE and some CJN people did a pitch to liberalize Reclaim Power and take out the civil disobedience. This was rejected, and FOE withdrew from CJA. After the March meeting, there were also some old-school autonomous groups that realized that CJA wasn't going to organize militant actions. So they withdrew to form NTAC ... But basically Reclaim Power was aimed at the middle, and that meant losing groups on the right and on the left.

(Interview, Climate Justice Action 2010)

---

[5] "Diversity of tactics" is a principle strongly associated with organizing in the global justice movement. The idea is that groups agree not to condemn one another's tactics, which may range from the purely nonviolent (peaceful protest) to the more violent end of the spectrum (usually meaning property damage).

Both NTAC and FOE-I formally left CJA, while continuing to send representatives to meetings. This example illustrates how strategic choices within the climate justice movement were "aimed at the middle," which meant losing support from both the more moderate and more radical ends of the spectrum.

MECHANISMS OF DECISION MAKING

The previous sections described the formation of the two main climate justice coalitions and the process by which these coalitions make tactical and framing decisions. But what about the organizations that work within them? How did they make important decisions during this time period? As in the previous chapter, my interview data suggest that relational mechanisms of decision making were particularly important for organizations that decided to adopt contentious forms of collective action. These groups frequently reported sharing information, pooling resources, and being influenced by one another. While some organizations did report that they made decisions based on prior ideological commitments, others suggested that the link between ideology and tactics was more fluid. This section summarizes my interview data.

RELATIONAL MECHANISMS

Relational dynamics were critical in the organization of contentious action. Most of the organizations originally involved in the coalition knew little about climate change, and even less about the UNFCCC. Part of the goal of the early CJA meetings was to explain the political process and how it worked. As a result of getting information from a common source, these organizations developed a common perception of the workings of political institutions and opportunities for access to them.

This information was not necessarily accurate or comprehensive. These organizations were often less aware of the potential range of targets for their actions and the opportunities for participation they afforded. As one member of Rising Tide explained, the perception of opportunities matters a great deal in the selection of targets for action within these groups, but the process of identifying opportunities is not very systematic:

In general, we tend to come and go with the opportunities that are available to us. So we might know that there is a shareholder meeting coming up, or an election, or a day of action and we would want to do something for that. But there's not always the greatest coherence to it – it tends to be kind of ad hoc. And it's really based on how much individuals know about what is going on and what they bring to the table.

(Interview, Rising Tide UK 2009)

In interviews, contentious groups commonly discussed how they found out about opportunities from their peers. For example, a number of organizations that met at the CJA meetings began to follow the practices of the major energy company Vattenfall in spring 2009. These organizations shared information about the timing of the company's public events and demonstration projects in the planning of protest actions. These groups were generally not as informed as their conventional counterparts about the operating of the UN system. It became clear in discussions that contentious groups tended to view the UNFCCC as analogous to an international financial institution, making them less likely to perceive meaningful political opportunities for activism within it.

Contentious organizations also often reported learning about new forms of collective action from their peers. The climate camps were crucial for this kind of tactical diffusion. Many of the practical skills associated with organizing blockades, occupations, and nonviolent civil disobedience were taught to activists at these camps. For example, at the UK Climate Camp in the summer of 2009, activists assembled in a field to practice marching in various formations to avoid police maneuvers that might stop them on their way. Activists attending the Dutch/Belgian Climate Camp could learn how to assemble tripods, how to use concrete lock-ons effectively, and how to scale a fence. At all the camps, some sessions focused on how to conduct political research into corporations and their lobbying practices. Individuals trained at these sessions could – and often reported that they did – bring this information back to their own organizations, expanding that group's tactical repertoire.

Finally, interorganizational contacts were important for learning what other organizations planned to do. This was particularly important going into Copenhagen. Learning that others intended to use contentious protest action lowered the costs of using the same form of action and made joining the "bandwagon" more appealing. As one group explained:

> We look to alliances to build momentum. These can be temporal – some are for one event, some for one month, one year, whatever. It depends a lot on the situation. But in principle, we don't want to be out on the streets alone [laughs] – we want to be out there with our allies, so they can't ignore us!
>
> (Interview, Ecologistas en Acción 2009)

Organizations did not have to sponsor CJA actions to be influenced by them. For example, representatives of Friends of the Earth and Attac attended CJA meetings regularly from the beginning of the process. As one participant described it, "in some sense, CJA was also a space for conversation" (Interview, Friends of the Earth France 2009). The knowledge that there would be a big, confrontational demonstration may have changed these organizations' action plans as well: both ended up significantly radicalizing their earlier plans. This exposure to information about CJA may have been critical to their decision, as they did not want to seem too tame in the eyes of their members or the media.

Nor did organizations' individually held resources hold them back from organizing contentious collective action. Groups frequently pooled their resources to create larger events and different kinds of actions than they were able to do alone. Coordinating logistics for Copenhagen was one of the original reasons for CJA's creation. Local Danish groups such as Klimax and the Climate Collective took on a great deal of the responsibility for finding places for activists to sleep in warehouses, army barracks, schools, and people's homes. They also organized communal kitchens and legal aid services. All of this made it more attractive for non-Danish groups to come to Copenhagen for the ultimate event. Groups from other regions also pooled their resources to sponsor buses traveling to the protest itself. The structure of support for these services was based on pledging, whereby organizations that had more funding paid more, and poorer organizations paid much less.

Organizations frequently cited the importance of ties and resources in convincing them to join the mobilization. For example, one participant explained the importance of the Climate Justice Caravan – a cross-Europe tour of speaking engagements and protest actions leading up to the Copenhagen Summit – to La Via Campesina's decision to get involved:

> This is why alliances are so important for us – what we're doing here is building social movements, and building support for the farmers whose livelihoods are at stake ... And our partners help not only with our analysis, but also to support large-scale public mobilizations like [Copenhagen] ... [The Copenhagen protest] was a mobilization in particular by groups who tried to discuss the climate issues as being more or less about trade ... So when we knew that people we worked with would be going, and we knew that they would organize a caravan to get there, we started to think that maybe we should get involved too.
>
> (Interview, La Via Campesina Europe 2009)

Groups that might not have been able to sponsor a protest were able to get involved as a result of resource pooling. A few small think tanks that became sponsors of protest actions leading up to the Copenhagen Summit provide a great example. These organizations were valuable to the coalition because they provided much needed political analysis. They were interested in participating themselves because it would give them access to other organizations' membership resources. As a member of staff at one think tank put it, talking to others convinced the organization that contentious action was not outside the realms of possibility for them:

> It was hard because for some groups they had never worked on this issue area before ... But we had been doing stuff on this for years, you know, making reports and the like. So for us, when people started talking to us about this movement and the action, we thought this is our chance to take it to the next level, yeah? And so maybe there is something we can contribute after all.
>
> (Interview, The Transnational Institute 2009)

The experience of organizing CJA also demonstrates that groups can be influenced and persuaded by their peers to adopt contentious forms of collective action. It was clear that influence went both ways within CJA: some organizations became more moderate than their original proposals indicated, and others became more radical. The ultimate result was a harmonization of tactics, with many organizations adopting contentious forms of action for the first time and using them before, during, and after Copenhagen. As one participant put it:

> At the CJA meeting in June ... some people were still uncomfortable about the direct action component. But at that point, a lot of Germans – mostly people who were formerly involved in the Peoples Global Action network and the G8 network[6] – pushed and gained dominance within CJA, and they convinced other people to go along with this idea. And so some of us really changed our plans.
>
> (Interview, European Youth for Action 2009)

The efforts of the global justice groups persuaded many organizations that direct action was the way to go. But many of the more radical groups eventually gave up the part of the action that involved shutting down the summit itself in order to participate in CJA. This example illustrates how ties to other groups can help change opinions as to what constitutes desirable and appropriate behavior. It also shows how organizational identity can change or be in flux when patterns of ties are disrupted and cherished forms of action are discarded in favor of new ones. As one activist described the process:

> For about half a year me and German colleagues tried to get CJA to have a position to shut down the COP. But once Via Campesina got involved, they said that CJA couldn't shut down the COP altogether – it would also be shutting down all the conversations that happen on the inside. And Via Campesina, I mean you know, they are one of the most democratic and legitimate organizations in the world. So from that point on, we knew that it had to be something different. So I think that was

---

[6] Both the Peoples' Global Action network and the G8 network are associated with organizing anti-summit protests and are important organizing vehicles in the European global justice movement.

one really good thing about the CJA mobilization – there was a lot of discussion, a lot of mutual learning. We couldn't just say "all institutions are the same, all governments suck." And because of that, for a lot of us on the radical left, it pushed us out of our comfort zone.

(Interview, Climate Camp Germany 2009)

Some organizations seemed to hold more sway in the coalition than others. My observation at many CJA meetings was that more experienced activists (who often had a background of summit protesting) held a higher status in the group and thus were capable of greater influence. Consensus decision making privileges skills of persuasion,[7] and those with more experience knew how to use the process to their benefit. Organizations capable of mobilizing large numbers of people were also closely listened to. Many organizations ultimately deferred to the opinions of groups representing the global south – such as La Via Campesina – because they believed that these organizations had a greater claim to legitimacy in the political discussion.

Ideological Constraint

However, my interviews suggest that a segment of the contentious population was constrained in its choice of action form by prior ideological commitments. I specifically find that groups coming from eco-anarchist backgrounds tend to be categorically opposed to lobbying actions. As one Rising Tide member put it:

One of our defining features is that we don't do lobbying. So others will do an occupation of a government office or another target, and we won't even do that. We try to focus on corporate targets instead, and particularly big oil. [JH: Why don't you do lobbying?] Well, I guess it all comes back to our underlying autonomous philosophy. We believe that the government doesn't have the power to make real changes because they are beholden to corporate interests. So we try to focus on the real source of the problem.

(Interview, Rising Tide 2009)

---

[7] It also seemed clear that those who were best able to communicate in English (not necessarily native speakers) held an advantage in the process.

But the link between ideology and tactics was less iron-clad for other groups. A representative from Attac explained the relationship between ideology and tactics as fluid and subject to social influence:

[JH: Why did you decide not to lobby?] We didn't decide not to lobby, we just didn't decide to do it. At the beginning it was clear that we wanted to do something together, but we just didn't know what … And many people in the coalition have a long experience with demonstrations and believe in the power of them. So I guess they were able to convince the others that that's what we should do … It is a strength that the coalition is so broad. [Attac is] radical in our ideology, but that doesn't necessarily imply that we will be radical in our methods.

(Interview, Attac France 2009)

This quote illustrates that ideologically radical groups were not necessarily constrained in their tactical choices when working within CJA. It is clear from my interviews and from the statistical analysis in Chapter 3 that while a significant subgroup of organizations did have a strong preference for contentious action from the outset, relational factors were critical in the ultimate choice of tactics.

Overall, the findings from the qualitative data lend validity to the correlations I discussed in Chapter 3. My qualitative data suggest that the process of tie formation is not driven by tactical homophily. Network ties are important because organizations are supporting and influencing one another in the use of certain forms of action. Many groups report that professionalization encourages moderation, but the fact that there are major exceptions such as Friends of the Earth suggests why variables measuring number of staff and budget source are not significant.[8] Having a radical ideology is a

---

[8] The FOE-I experience may demonstrate that it is not institutionalization per se that leads to tactical moderation, but the way in which an organization decides to institutionalize. The decentralization of the organization had important consequences for decision making within Friends of the Earth (see Doherty and Doyle 2013).

strong predictor of engaging in contentious action, because many eco-anarchist groups are constrained ideologically. Changes in political opportunities are a significant predictor of contentious action because conventional groups tend to rationally evaluate political opportunities, as Chapter 4 suggests.

Contentious groups perceived opportunities in ways that differed systematically from conventional groups. They systematically shared information, analysis, and strategy within their social circles in a way that predisposed them toward more radical forms of action and new ways of framing issues. These groups made intentional decisions to form contentious enclaves, which helped them maintain their political analysis and promote their preferred tactics. The next chapter considers the implications of these developments for the politics of climate change.

CONCLUSION

Virtually all of the contentious actions described in this chapter emerged from interorganizational bargaining and persuasion among diverse groups. The ultimate consensus was difficult for some to support. One described his ambivalence:

I feel that the movement is both hopeful and hopeless: we don't believe our leaders can solve the crisis. But we also don't totally believe in the movement yet either. We are working within the frame given to us by the Copenhagen Summit because we are desperate. And I worry that that means we are not dealing with the climate crisis, but we are dealing with how the climate crisis is dealt with.

(Interview, Climate Camp Germany 2009)

Groups within Climate Justice Action were successful in persuading others to adopt contentious tactics. Through the coalition, organizations shared information with one another, pooled important resources, and developed new tactics and issue frames. Friends of the Earth's decision to leave illustrates both the volatility of the negotiations within CJA and the seriousness with which organizations weigh their strategic options.

This chapter documented the emergence of climate justice politics. I argue that much radical activism in the climate change movement emerged from the milieu of global justice politics and, as a result, its frames and tactics were adapted from the repertoire of this earlier movement. Climate justice groups formed alliances with a group of dissatisfied organizations working inside the negotiations. Together, they engaged in significant outreach to other groups and successfully convinced many others to adopt a contentious climate justice approach.

This chapter also illustrated how relational mechanisms influenced decision making regarding tactical options. Like Polletta's (2002) study of the internal debates of the Direct Action Network in New York and Juris's (2008) ethnography of the global justice movement in Europe, my research shows how differences are negotiated and accommodated among diverse actors, and how collective action emerges in such a setting. The next chapter deals with a bigger question: What is the impact of civil society activism? I argue that the emergence of contentious collective action – and its lack of connection to conventional advocacy – had important implications for climate change politics.

6

Implications for Climate Change Politics

So far, I have argued that the network of civil society actors became significantly larger, more diverse, and more divided in the buildup to the Copenhagen Summit. This chapter traces the implications of those developments for climate change politics more broadly. In previous chapters I explained how the growing diversity of groups supported a wider range of tactics than had been previously employed: this resulted in an unprecedented expansion in contention around the UNFCCC in 2009, as I will document here. Changes in civil society participation transformed the UNFCCC from an off-the-radar venue for expert advocacy to a high-profile target of activism. Earth Negotiations Bulletin described this development in 2011:

> Climate change COPs have evolved into a carnival-like forum ... with a dizzying array of events competing for attention and mindshare. From side events, displays of green technology, marches and protests, to real time commentary over the internet through Twitter, Facebook and thousands of blogs, civil society [meetings] are something that a transparent COP host has to manage.
>
> (Earth Negotiations Bulletin 2011)

In this chapter, I argue that these changes in civil society tactics have caused the UNFCCC to become more restrictive in its policing and to seek reform in its procedures for dealing with civil society groups more generally.

I noted in previous chapters how the involvement of a wider range of groups introduced a new way of framing climate change as an issue of climate justice. This approach contrasted with the traditional frame of scientific urgency previously employed by most civil society groups. In this chapter, I examine the success of this frame. I find that the media, states, and other civil society groups have adopted the language of climate justice. I also argue that the frame diffusion has inspired new cleavages in the inter-state politics of climate change, as well as a potential, if fragile, convergence in civil society.

This chapter employs the technique of process tracing to demonstrate how changes in civil society activity can influence political outcomes (Betsill and Corell 2001; Zürn 1998). I focus on two changes – increased use of contentious tactics and deployment of the climate justice frame – and trace the implications for climate change politics more broadly. I draw on a range of sources – including media accounts, interviews, institutional documents, and speeches – to provide evidence of the political impact of civil society strategies. I specifically document how the use of climate justice framing and contentious activism changed language, policy, and institutions around global climate governance. While noting that my scope is limited by my focus on only two developments within civil society and within the limited time span of this study, I conclude by considering what this case can tell us about the future of global climate politics.

THE UNFCCC AS A TARGET OF CONTENTIOUS ACTIVISM

Previous chapters documented how and why a growing number of civil society groups decided to adopt contentious forms of collective action in advance of the Copenhagen Summit. This chapter draws on quantitative protest event analysis to show that the culmination of their individual decisions produced an unprecedented amount of contention. Not only did the Copenhagen meeting feature the largest number of protest events on climate change ever recorded; these events also drew a massive number of participants and were much more likely to be transgressive in character than those at previous meetings.

Protest event analysis is a method for collecting systematic longitudinal data on contentious events through coding of news sources. For this project, I employed traditional protest event analysis of newspaper sources alongside coding of issue-specific daily newsletters. First, I conducted an extensive search of media sources in the LexisNexis database for each COP from 2005 to 2013, limiting my search to reports filed in the city in which the COP was held.[1] Because of the high number of false positives returned with the general search terms, each of the news items was hand-coded to determine whether or not it contained a relevant contentious action related to the COP. These data complement those presented in Chapter 3 by examining the volume of UN climate protest over a longer time period. The results were used to assess the relative frequency of protest, as shown in Figure 6.1.

First, these data show us that the number of protest events in Copenhagen was truly unprecedented, with a record number of seventy-seven protest events around this meeting. Most UNFCCC meetings – including the 2005, 2007, 2008, 2010, and 2011 COPs – attracted approximately 10–25 protests each. More technical meetings – including those in 2006, 2012, and 2013 – experienced virtually no civil society protests. These data capture the frequency of protest events, however, not their size or significance. For example, while the 2013 COP in Warsaw was the site of a few dramatic protest events, including a civil society walkout on the negotiations and a high-profile hunger strike, the data show us that there were numerically fewer protest events around this conference than in previous years.

---

[1] Specifically, I searched for the terms "(climate change or global warming) AND (UN or United Nations) AND (protest* or march* or demonstrat*)." While the addition of independent media sources would be ideal, this type of reporting is not systematically available for the entire time period of the study. More details of this research procedure are contained in the Methods Appendix.

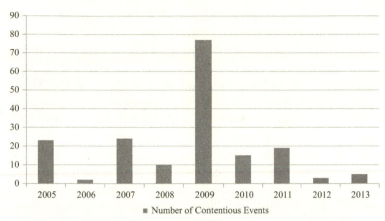

FIGURE 6.1. Number of Contentious Events Reported during COP, 2005–13

Some scholars have critiqued protest analysis for being vulnerable to reporting bias, meaning that the amount of protest reported could well be a function of the amount of coverage of climate change overall (Koopmans and Rucht 2002). Reporting bias can be difficult to detect using media sources alone, because high-profile meetings attract both more coverage and more protest. To assess the extent of this bias, I coded a different kind of publication – Earth Negotiations Bulletin (ENB) – which provides comprehensive daily coverage of the official UNFCCC negotiations. Since this publication has consistent coverage, it is likely to have more limited reporting bias. Analysis of this publication supports the results from my coding of newspaper sources: protests were uncommon at most COPs, and the correlation between the number of events reported for each COP from the ENB and the LexisNexis sources was 0.91. The combination of these converging sources and the evidence presented in previous chapters should make us more confident that these data reflect a genuine expansion in contention.

Second, the scale of these protest events in Copenhagen was simply much larger. Fisher (2004) estimates there were approximately 5,000 protesters at the UNFCCC meeting in 2000, but in

2009 there was a massive demonstration of 100,000 people, as well as many smaller protest events (Fisher 2010). A total of over 13,000 individuals registered with the United Nations to lobby their delegates and observe the negotiations, while 17 million people signed an online petition demanding urgent action. More than a half million activists in 140 countries participated in coordinated demonstrations on the Global Day of Climate Action. Although comparable data from earlier years are not available, research teams collecting individual-level data at this protest confirm that the majority of individual participants were aware of the transnational dimensions of the mobilization, making this a highly significant transnational protest event (Walgrave et al. 2012; see also Wahlstrom, Wennerhag, and Rootes 2013).

Finally, the character of these events shifted in Copenhagen. Before 2009, most of the (limited) protest that occurred around the UNFCCC was of a nonthreatening character: examples might include the nonviolent activist demonstration in Poznan in 2008 or the march of activists wearing polar bear costumes in Bali in 2007. These are the kind of media-friendly stunts that members of CAN typically sponsored around climate negotiations. But Copenhagen marked the emergence of a more confrontational and transgressive repertoire of climate change activism, which had previously been rare.

Theoretically, transgressive contention is a subset of contentious action that can be distinguished because it comes from new actors who disrupt established routines in their protest actions (McAdam, Tarrow, and Tilly 2001, 7). There are two crucial differences between the transgressive protest at Copenhagen and earlier protest actions. First, contentious events at the UNFCCC have usually been mobilized in support of stronger climate policy from the UNFCCC (Fisher 2004). Second, these protests have typically been sponsored by the same ENGO activists who were organizing actions inside the UNFCCC, and function as a small complement to their lobbying work. In Copenhagen, transgressive actions often came from newly mobilized actors and tended to be highly confrontational in language and demands.

One example of transgressive activism is the Reclaim Power action discussed in Chapter 5. As I documented, many activists began to call for the use of summit protest tactics against the UNFCCC in the buildup to Copenhagen. The summit protest is a well-known component of the global justice movement's repertoire. As Wood (2007) argues, the Seattle tactics associated with summit protests include four elements: affinity groups; black bloc; jail solidarity; and protest puppetry. Yet these elements had not been used previously in climate politics, and this explains why the emergence of these transgressive actions caused particular uncertainty and upheaval in the politics of the UNFCCC. I will go on to discuss the implications of this tactical shift.

Even though most COPs I examined featured little transgressive activism, it is worth noting that this type of protest did appear forcefully at the 2000 COP in The Hague. Protesters at this meeting also made aggressive attempts to disrupt the institutional functioning of the UNFCCC, including storming the building, throwing paint bombs at buildings, climbing rafters, and destroying electrical equipment. One protester threw a custard pie in the face of U.S. Chief Delegate Frank Loy to express anger over the lack of U.S. action on climate change. But as UNFCCC Security responded aggressively to these protests, many mainstream groups (in particular Greenpeace) made efforts to disassociate themselves from these actions. These tactics were largely disowned within the NGO community, and while contentious events took place at subsequent COPs, few had the same transgressive character until Copenhagen.

INSTITUTIONAL RESPONSE: A MORE RESTRICTIVE UNFCCC

How do institutions respond to protest, especially protest that is transgressive in nature? Intuitively, we might expect that a great volume of protest would increase the chances that civil society groups would achieve their desired ends. Many activists hold this mental model. But studies of the global justice movement have also documented another outcome of transgressive protest:

increased restrictions and policing (della Porta 2007b; O'Neill 2004; Wood 2007). The UNFCCC seems to fit this pattern as well: it has long prided itself on its openness to civil society but, in the years since Copenhagen, has responded to growing contention by becoming more restrictive in terms of access and policing.

The closing off of political opportunities at the UNFCCC can be seen in three respects. First, security around the conference became stricter and more proactive in targeting potential threats as indications of contentious activism increased. According to my protest event analysis, from 2005 to 2008, virtually no events that attracted police intervention were reported. In 2009, seventeen events (22 percent) resulted in arrests. Security forces used tear gas, beatings with batons, and mass arrests to contain protesters at this meeting. The number of arrests was also unprecedented: newspaper accounts place it at somewhere around 3,000 protesters in total. Even as the overall level of protest has dramatically decreased, 20 percent of events in Cancun, 32 percent in Durban, and 33 percent in Doha resulted in arrests. Activists report that security officials have been much more proactive, aggressive, and restrictive in policing protest actions around subsequent COPs (Interview, Climate Action Network International 2011). Although this is not a systematic study of policing practices, these observations suggest that changes in the repertoire of contention stimulated changes in policing around the COPs.

Second, security concerns contributed to an unprecedented decision by the UNFCCC to severely restrict access to the venue for the final days of Copenhagen. An email from the UNFCCC Civil Society Liaison stated that for "safety and security reasons," only ninety of the 13,000 civil society observers present would be permitted into the venue on the final Thursday and Friday when world leaders would be present. Civil society representatives, who had flown in from all over the world for the meeting, were outraged. Thus, most civil society groups had virtually no access to the UNFCCC venue during one of the most important conferences in its history.

These strict restrictions were clearly a response to the appearance of transgressive protest. The fact that the UNFCCC Security
Team particularly targeted Friends of the Earth, completely revok-
ing the accreditation of all 300 members of the group days before
the rest of civil society was shut out, supports this interpretation.
FOE leaders reported in interviews that they were told their group
had been identified as a threat in a UNFCCC security report, but
that the UN Security Team had declined to elaborate on the reasons
why. Previous chapters have noted that FOE was an important
bridge between the more contentious actors and the mainstream
NGOs. Other civil society groups – including CAN – appealed to
the Secretariat to have FOE reinstated, but to no avail.

Increased security restrictions were not limited to Copenhagen.
Security procedures were even stricter in Cancun in 2010, despite
the almost complete absence of heads of state. In Copenhagen,
actions were permitted if cleared with the Secretariat. In Cancun,
UN security imposed a two-day waiting period for any civil society
action, effectively curtailing civil society's ability to respond to
events in the negotiations in a timely manner. UN security was
active in removing individuals who took part in protest actions
in Cancun. Activists noted that they did this by either noting
participants' names from their badges or reviewing footage of
protests and matching faces with photos in the registration system.
One prominent indigenous activist described his suspension from
the UNFCCC in this way:

We took our delegation over to the U.N. forum and went through the
security and swiped my – this card here. And all of a sudden, the whole
computer started flashing red. I was suspended ... So we found out that
because yesterday we were talking yesterday after a press conference ...
after that, our youth went out, you know, demanding climate justice and
to lift up all the issues that we're addressing ... So, of course, the media
was asking, you know, what is the indigenous position on this? So
I spoke, as well ... And I didn't know there was anything that we were
doing wrong at all.

(Goldtooth 2010)

The targeting of individuals is a new phenomenon in the
UNFCCC's security arrangements. The UNFCCC had previously

preferred to rely on a group-sanctioning policy, counting on organizations to restrain their members. The extent to which this policy will be used on a permanent basis is still unknown; however, one can reason that suspending individuals will give the UNFCCC more leverage in removing individual protesters from the talks without having to justifying bans on entire organizations. On the other hand, if the group-sanctioning policy is weakened, organizations will have fewer incentives to rein in contentious individuals, potentially lowering the costs of individuals engaging in protest actions.

The Durban negotiations in 2012 were similarly marked by unclear rules about which actions were acceptable and which were not. Participants reported that while the South African government demonstrated commitment to open access and consultation, the UN Security Team acted particularly "by the book" and was strict in shutting down actions. As a result, the conference was marked by a number of Occupy-style actions that led to extensive removals of participants from the venue (Interview, Climate Action Network 2012). The severely limited space for protest in Dubai "was a major source of concern" for civil society representatives attending the 2012 COP; this began a process of reflection that contributed to a decision to walk out at the 2013 meeting in Warsaw (Interview, Oxfam International 2013).

Third, civil society groups have been put on guard by discussions within the UNFCCC itself regarding reform in participation. The Aarhus Convention Secretariat report on COP 15 noted that an "atmosphere of distrust" had grown between civil society and the institution and that there was a need to "rebuild the dialogue" (United Nations Economic Commission for Europe 2010). The UNFCCC began a process within the Subsidiary Body on Implementation (SBI) to look into ways to "enhance observer participation" as a result of this growing dissatisfaction. This has been an intricate process. The UNFCCC clearly favors conventional participation while eschewing protest, explaining that civil society participation "flourishes in an atmosphere of mutual trust which acknowledges respect for others and their opinions, and takes into account the nature of intergovernmental sessions" (United Nations Framework Convention on Climate Change 2010, 3). This attitude has led many civil society groups to fear that any eventual reform may stifle their right to dissent.

The UNFCCC's reevaluation of civil society participation came amid increased state skepticism about its value. Civil society groups approached the SBI discussion by asking for increased access to meetings, interventions, and documents, but several proposals from states suggested creating separate venues for civil society participation that would preclude the need for NGOs to participate directly in the COPs. For example, one proposal in this body suggested establishing a pre-COP high-level NGO dialogue that would mandate venues for civil society participation that would be entirely separate from the COPs themselves. NGO delegates strongly objected to this, on the grounds that it would "tokenize" their participation under the guise of "enhanced participation" (CAN 2010). While these proposals are unlikely to take hold, civil society groups are increasingly on guard in this arena and concerned that their once abundant access may be much more strictly limited at future sessions.

A LARGER ROLE FOR JUSTICE IN THE POLITICS OF CLIMATE CHANGE

The second big change in Copenhagen was that civil society groups developed a new way to talk about climate change. Scholars have already documented that civil society groups can change how environmental issues are discussed (Betsill and Corell 2001; Gulbrandsen and Andresen 2004). Drawing on original evidence, I find indications of this discursive impact in climate change politics and demonstrate that after its development and promotion by civil society actors, the climate justice lens was adopted widely in the media, by a number of state delegates, and by other civil society groups. I detail each of these outcomes in this section.

First, civil society groups often try to influence the media with their statements and actions. My analysis suggests that this

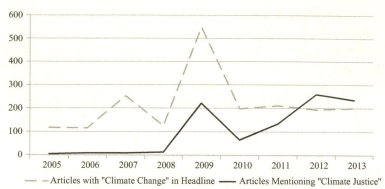

— — Articles with "Climate Change" in Headline   —— Articles Mentioning "Climate Justice"

FIGURE 6.2. Media Use of the Term "Climate Justice," 2005–13

strategy worked for the climate justice movement: the media have increasingly employed climate justice language since the 2009 meeting. To get a sense of this trend in media coverage, I conducted a simple search of the LexisNexis database for newspaper articles that employed the term "climate justice" in a given year.[2] Figure 6.2 plots the use of the term. For reference, I included a second trend line with general coverage of climate change COPs from 2005 to 2011.

As Figure 6.2 shows, the popularity of the phrase took off after 2008. According to these data, only five articles used the term in 2005, but the term appeared in 221 newspaper articles in 2009. Although the figures do drop off a bit in the immediate aftermath of Copenhagen, the term is still used in more than 200 articles in both 2012 and 2013. As the figure suggests, much of the decrease in the use of the term might be because the climate issue was generally less salient to the media after 2009. The recent increase in usage indicates that climate justice is becoming a popular lens despite stagnating media interest. I would speculate that reporters were likely attracted to the climate justice

---

[2] For the general climate coverage search, the specific search terms used were (climate change or global warming) AND (UN or United Nations) AND HEADLINE((climate change or global warming)) for the date range of each COP, within the LexisNexis database, drawing on newspaper sources.

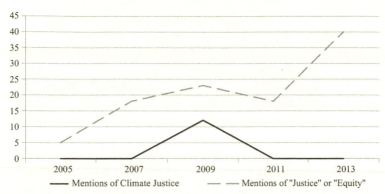

FIGURE 6.3. Use of "Climate Justice" and Associated Terms by States in UNFCCC Speeches, 2005–13

frame for the same reason as activists: the simplicity of the frame helps pitch complicated stories in an emotionally resonant way. Moreover, the disruptive tactics often associated with the movement likely drew reporters (and coverage), further educating the media about this movement and its demands.

Second, civil society groups often try to influence state leaders directly, as climate justice activists did in 2009. Were they successful? My results suggest that activists had at least a short-term influence on the ways in which state leaders discussed climate politics. I established this influence by documenting that state leaders adopted the language of climate justice for the first time in Copenhagen. I coded floor speeches given by heads of states at the high-level segment of climate change conferences in 2005, 2007, 2009, 2011, and 2013 to capture this dynamic.[3] These speeches are a good source of data because they are relatively uniform in length and give us a sense of the issues that world leaders choose to prioritize. Figure 6.3 presents these data.

This analysis shows that 2009 was the only year in which the specific term "climate justice" appeared in delegate speeches. The term did not appear at all in 2005 or 2007, but twelve state delegates employed it in 2009. This suggests

---

[3] The Methods Appendix describes this procedure further.

the direct influence of the movement at this conference, and the success of these outreach efforts.

What about the years after Copenhagen? The climate justice movement has not focused as much on direct outreach to states in the UNFCCC as it did during Copenhagen. But it is notable that even though the use of "climate justice" as a specific phrase has disappeared, states are paying more attention to broader equity and justice issues. Twenty-three states (about 15 percent of those speaking) employed these terms at the Copenhagen conference. At the most recent conference in Warsaw, this figure increased to forty states (about 32 percent of those speaking).[4] Although it is harder to attribute these changes to direct influence, it is clear that as the broader context of these negotiations has changed, the prominence of the issues associated with climate justice has also increased.

Finally, civil society groups often vie with one another for influence. I find significant evidence that the development of the climate justice frame has influenced the ways in which mainstream environmental groups have begun to frame climate change. To capture this change in framing, I coded all issues of the Climate Action Network's newsletter *ECO* from 2005 to 2013. This newsletter is published on each day of the negotiations and is an important channel of communication for CAN during the COPs. Drawing on the coding scheme described in the Methods Appendix, I coded each issue for the number of times a science-based or justice-equity framing was employed. Figure 6.4 represents these data.

These data show that CAN has moved away from its traditional scientific approach and has increasingly embraced an issue framing that focuses on equity and justice issues. Whereas this trend is evident from 2007 to 2009, it is particularly remarkable post-2009, when the use of scientific framing declines dramatically relative to the justice and equity approach. This offers quite plausible evidence that the discursive influence of the climate

---

[4] At the time of writing, not all of the speeches from COP 19 were available online. Those that were have been coded and are presented here.

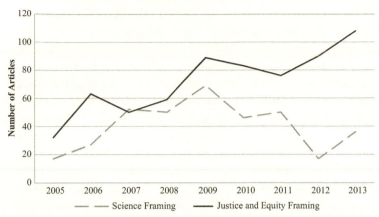

FIGURE 6.4. Frame Analysis of Articles in CAN's *ECO* Newsletter, 2005–13

justice movement has extended to other non-state actors. I also note that CAN's strategic change is not a straightforward imitation of the framing strategy of the climate justice movement. CAN still tends to prefer the term "equity" to "justice," suggesting a continued insider emphasis. I discuss the implications of this development later in this chapter.

So far, I have demonstrated that changes in the nature of civil society participation – specifically the increased use of contentious tactics and climate justice framing – influenced the language and policy of institutions, media, states, and other civil society groups. But what does this mean for cooperation on climate change? The next two sections explore the implications of these developments for alliances in interstate politics, as well as for the internal politics of civil society.

NEW CLEAVAGES IN GLOBAL CLIMATE
NEGOTIATIONS

The climate justice approach encompasses a broader set of priorities and a new attention to the process of political negotiations. At the time of Copenhagen, the introduction of the climate justice

perspective initiated a new cleavage into the global climate negotiations. The climate justice approach differed from the approach
of mainstream environmental groups in three areas. First, the
climate justice approach highlighted different priorities – those
associated with justice in mitigation and adaptation commitments – than mainstream environmental groups. While environmental groups may have often shared these commitments, they
tended to prioritize the development of an environmentally
sound climate treaty as the most important outcome. Second,
climate justice activists routinely stated that "no deal is better
than a bad deal" and encouraged states to block deals that would
not achieve just outcomes. This contrasts with traditional NGOs,
which in Copenhagen were pushing to "Seal the Deal." Third,
the two sides of the network had different time horizons: reform-
oriented NGOs pushed the scientific urgency of the climate issue,
while climate justice groups were willing to allow the need to
slow down in order to get the political process right. As a result,
the climate justice groups often ended up pushing for different
agendas within the talks, introducing new elements of contestation to the already turbulent negotiations.

The two sides of the network cultivated different state allies at
the 2009 summit. A core part of the Climate Action Network's
strategy in Copenhagen was to build an international civil society
network that would have strong domestic groups located all over
the globe. CAN hoped that these domestic groups would put
pressure on their delegations, in the context of the international
negotiations, to achieve an ambitious agreement. Daily CAN
meetings – like those of other major international environmental
NGOs – consisted of campaigners putting together the puzzle
pieces from all of the feedback from domestic groups to figure
out how best to leverage their connections to influence the trajectory of the talks.

But climate justice groups pursued a different approach. A key
part of their strategy for Copenhagen (and beyond) was to target
key states that might be willing to block negotiations that would
not achieve just outcomes. As a result, the scope of this advocacy
did not need to be global: in the context of the UNFCCC's

consensus negotiations, it would be enough to have a small handful of states that were willing to oppose any proposed agreement. As Young (1994, 109) argues, in situations in which consensus rules operate, "the availability of arrangements that all participants can accept as equitable is necessary for institutional bargaining to succeed." Climate justice activists hoped to replicate the experience of the 1999 Seattle World Trade Organization meeting, in which outsider activist organizations were credited with supporting the dissent of developing country delegations participating in the talks (Edelman 2009). As an early organizing document put it:

> In Seattle, we not only managed to shut down the conference by being on the streets, we also exacerbated the multiple conflicts that existed "on the inside" between the negotiating governments ... If we manage to do the same thing again ... we would be able to keep open the political space to discuss potential "solutions" to climate change that go beyond the reigning, market-driven agenda.
>
> (Müller 2008)

Putting this strategy into action required getting the message across to key state delegates. This task was made easier because many state delegates from the Bolivarian Alliance for the Peoples of Our America (ALBA) countries of Latin America were already quite receptive to the message. Many of the ALBA delegations to the UNFCCC intentionally included a large number of social movement and indigenous participants who had existing social movement ties. The boundaries between these delegates and the climate justice movement were sometimes porous. Participants in the Reclaim Power demonstration described in Chapter 5 often explained their motivation as reflecting a desire to support critical states within the negotiations. As one participant from the Indigenous Environmental Network shouted upon leaving the conference center: "We are here to support our brothers. We are here to support Evo Morales; he is coming here today. We are here to give him direction and to support Bolivia" (Democracy Now 2009).

ALBA leaders seemed to be listening, and their delegations actively consulted and coordinated with climate justice activists in Copenhagen. One example of this coordination was Evo

Morales' decision to spend a full day of his time in Copenhagen attending the Klimaforum, as opposed to the official UNFCCC conference. Morales offered to present the official declaration of the Klimaforum to the UNFCCC. Although this never happened (the UNFCCC Secretariat reportedly stated that the document was "lost"), it signaled the extent of overlap and collaboration between the climate justice movement and the Bolivian state. As Morales explained in a public speech in Copenhagen:

> Politics is a science of serving the people. I live to serve the people. Participating in politics is part of assuring our dignity, our traditional way of life. It is my duty to take your message to the heads of state here. If I make a mistake, let me know so that I can rectify it.
>
> (Morales 2009)

After contact with the climate justice movement, ALBA leaders increasingly began to employ climate justice rhetoric and to draw on the protest movements as a source of legitimacy for their political positioning. In contrast to their statements at earlier summits, they explicitly mentioned protests and climate justice slogans (e.g., "system change, not climate change") and used them to support and justify their opposition to the UN process. This was particularly true in Hugo Chavez's floor speech:

> But there are lots of people outside too ... there are a lot of protests in the Copenhagen streets. I would like to say hello to all those people out there [applause] ... I was reading some signs out there is the street ... one, for example, is "don't change the climate, change the system." Don't change the climate, change the system. I take that; I take note of that. Let's change the system, and then we will begin to change the climate and save the world [applause].
>
> (Chavez 2009)

Other ALBA countries also adopted the rhetoric of the movement and criticized the UNFCCC for its harsh stance against civil society:

> I would like to associate myself with the protests and the demonstrations ... we note with concern the exclusion of non-governmental organizations from this hall, and the clear repressive measures being used against demonstrators ... selfishness and the

interests of developed countries in preserving an unjust and inequitable world order are preventing us from undertaking the changes that are demanded by present and future generations.

(Hernández 2009)

This use of climate justice language by heads of state was new in Copenhagen and promoted a perception of inequality in the talks. And while ALBA leaders were certainly predisposed toward these views, contact with the climate justice movement likely encouraged this change in discourse.

Beyond discourse, contact with the climate justice movement may have also influenced decision making about the Copenhagen Accord. The main opposition to the Accord came from a group of states that had already been associated with the climate justice movement. In particular, Bolivia, Cuba, Venezuela, and Nicaragua spoke early and strongly against the accord and the inequitable way in which they felt it was brokered (United Nations Framework Convention on Climate Change 2009b). These states, which had already been primed with climate justice discourse, were the ones mainly responsible for refusing to allow the Copenhagen Accord to become an official UNFCCC decision. The extensive overlap between the climate justice movement and the ALBA delegations makes it quite plausible that the activism encouraged some states to sustain their oppositional stance within the UNFCCC (McGregor 2010), even if it is impossible to definitively demonstrate.

At the very least, it is clear that these delegates were listening to contentious activists and using their actions as a way to legitimize their political positions. This is clear in the final statement put out by ALBA on the outcome of the Copenhagen Summit:

Today more than ever, before the lamentable maneuvering that has been practiced in Copenhagen for petty economic interests, we reiterate that, "Don't change the climate, change the system!"... We recall that while the conference failed in an irreversible way, the voices of the youth who know that the future is theirs, grows stronger. They strongly denounce the maneuvers of the developed countries and they know that the struggle will continue. We join with them and their protests, and we salute and support them. The people must stay on their guard.

(ALBA 2009)

These states also evaluated their actions by the standards set by civil society groups after Copenhagen. As Morales put it:

I would say that Copenhagen is not a failure, it is a success for the people, and a failure for the developed governments. Because in December 2009, the developed countries tried to approve a document, and thanks to the struggle of you, the leaders of social movements of the world meeting in Copenhagen, along with presidents of some countries, we communicated the feeling of suffering of the peoples of the world.

(Morales 2010)

Beyond Copenhagen, this experience has inspired ALBA leaders to pursue climate leadership in other venues. Notably, Bolivia sponsored a World People's Conference on Climate Change in 2010 that was meant to serve as a grassroots alternative to the top-down politics of the UNFCCC. The process and procedures of this meeting echo the politics of the World Social Forum, where the issue was also discussed subsequently. In many respects, the development of these new cleavages within the UNFCCC has emboldened some state leaders, but it has also been the impetus for the development of a broader and more critical social movement that is not exclusively aimed at the UN system. I consider the longer-term implications of this development in the Conclusion.

TOWARD A CONVERGENCE IN CIVIL SOCIETY?

The mobilization of the climate justice movement also has a large influence on other civil society groups working around the UNFCCC. This book has so far detailed the development of a significant cleavage between groups that was especially pronounced and consequential in 2009. But what happened in the years after this? The most recent evidence supports the idea of a limited convergence emerging among civil society groups, in three respects.

First, this chapter demonstrated that climate change organizations are increasingly framing their demands in terms of climate justice. Most environmental NGOs chose to mobilize using the scientific urgency frame in 2009, dividing them from the emerging climate justice movement. But by 2013, civil society groups seemed united around the climate justice approach, as my coding demonstrates. Even WWF, an organization thought to be at the more moderate end of the spectrum of environmental groups, employed climate justice language at the 2013 meeting. Second, notable reforms have occurred within the biggest interorganizational coalition – the Climate Action Network – that respond to critiques of the climate justice movement. Specifically, CAN has invested in its Southern Capacity Program to support groups located in developing countries, hired a new director from the Middle East, changed the nature of its leadership structure, and formed an equity committee to consider issues associated with differentiation and sequencing. All of these changes are described as originating from "demands from the members" that these issues be tackled by the coalition (Interview, Climate Action Network International 2013). Third, climate justice groups and CAN members collaborated on a significant joint contentious action at the 2013 meeting in Warsaw. Specifically, groups agreed to walk out of the talks en masse to demonstrate frustration with the lack of progress. While the demonstration was not highly confrontational, it signaled important cooperation between climate justice groups and the big NGOs, including Oxfam, WWF, Friends of the Earth, and Greenpeace. While these groups were divided at the time of Copenhagen, they seem increasingly open to bridging their divides.

What explains this change? A lot of the change seems to come from social influence among groups. For example, members of Climate Justice Now describe intentionally reaching out to CAN members about political positioning. As one explained, groups' receptivity to the climate justice approach post-Copenhagen was partially the result of the deterioration of the negotiations themselves:

The Doha text was so terrible: it locks in virtually no progress for seven years. And so some members – Friends of the Earth in particular – started to reach out to CAN and especially WWF and Oxfam. Suddenly they could agree that things were truly bad. So I think there was a lot of peer education that went on there about climate justice and what it means.

(Interview, CJN, 2013)

Another noted: "In Copenhagen CJN and CAN wanted nothing to do with one another. Now the dialogue is much more constructive" (Interview, Climate Justice Now, 2013).

Better coordination among groups is likely to bring about more effective actions. But one question often posed by activists is whether the broad diffusion of the climate justice frame might pose some risks. The success of the climate justice movement – and the increased prominence of its framing – represents an opportunity and a challenge for mainstream environmental NGOs. And, as one anonymous activist complained, this new framing hasn't necessarily led to the development of new policy: "The climate can't be fixed with capitalism ... And some big organizations claim to support climate justice, but also have trading foundations. It seems like the climate justice language is being hijacked and co-opted by big NGOs who want to fudge the differences in the climate justice movement." From this perspective, much of the bite of the climate justice frame comes from its engagement with an anticapitalist and antisystemic perspective. If the language of climate justice is watered down, then the corresponding political changes may also be less than transformational, and may co-opt the movement in significant ways.

But many take a more optimistic view of the potential for convergence without co-optation. As another campaigner explained, when asked if she was concerned about the climate justice movement being co-opted:

I think some groups take on climate justice without really thinking about it or knowing what it means. But a lot have listened and gone through a process of changing ... it seems like it has really been on our terms, with them coming to us.

(Interview, CJN, 2013)

This book establishes that social influence is a real force among organizations. As I note in the Introduction, network structure influences the frames and tactics that organizations adopt, but the adoption of frames and tactics can also restructure networks in critical ways. Coalescing around a common frame suggests the potential for future convergence in the network. And while this cohesion may be fragile at this point, its implications for the international climate movement could be highly significant.

CONCLUSION

The chapter shows that divisions in the climate network resulted in two big changes in civil society actors' participation in the Copenhagen Summit. First, their repertoire of climate change activism became much more contentious and confrontational. Second, many groups began to adopt and promote a climate justice lens in the negotiations. These were clearly not the only changes that took place in Copenhagen; however, I suggest they are two particularly important developments that had an important influence on the future trajectory of the movement and the political process within the UNFCCC.

It is clear from my analysis that the climate justice movement has been successful to date in developing a new and powerful approach to framing the climate issue. This frame has spread to a variety of actors, suggesting that framing power is an effective tool wielded by this movement. The discursive influence of the movement is particularly notable when one examines how it influenced other non-state actors. And while this is beyond the scope of this study, I consider it probable that this discursive influence has translated into policy influence in the case of some non-state actors and some states in the UNFCCC process.

This chapter suggests important pathways by which the mobilization of civil society affects the development of global climate politics, but it is important not to overstate the scope of this influence. Clearly, civil society groups did not get what they ultimately wanted in Copenhagen: an ambitious and fair climate treaty. While groups had an observable influence on some states, it is difficult to imagine that this strategy could be replicated with other major actors. Influence is real, but it is not unlimited. More systematic analysis of movement impacts is urgently needed to extend our understanding of this important topic.

I conclude this chapter by noting that the literature on transnational advocacy networks has been much criticized for its tendency to focus on successful cases of civil society activism (Price 2003). This study traces the impact of the mobilization of civil society actors, but it does not concentrate exclusively on whether or not they were successful in achieving their aims (see Busby 2010). Paying attention to the broader consequences of mobilization – including outcomes such as increased restrictions and policing – draws our attention to results that may be unexpected and even undesirable. These outcomes are understudied and especially deserving of attention as we attempt to develop a better grasp on the results of activism.

My analysis has examined the short- to medium-term implications of the climate network's mobilization. These outcomes are important, but I also note that NGOs can exert broader power than the outcomes I am able to examine here (Wapner 1995). The Conclusion considers the future of the international climate movement and its potential to achieve broader social change outside of the scope of this study.

Conclusion

As I write this book, climate change is regaining prominence on the international agenda. The emission of greenhouse gases continues unabated (Intergovernmental Panel on Climate Change 2013); United Nations Secretary-General Ban Ki-moon invited world leaders and heads of state to a special summit on climate change in September 2014; talks within the UNFCCC are aiming at a new negotiating deadline of 2015; and climate activists are having discussions about what to do at the next round of climate negotiations. They are reexamining their previous strategies and tactics. As a commentator in *The Guardian* boldly proclaimed after the Doha talks in 2012:

> The lessons from Copenhagen must be learned . . . Climate change needs to become again a moral crusade. Global warming is a theft of the future from the children of today: anger and emotion must galvanise public concern . . . the debate around a new global agreement needs to be driven from the south of the world, giving proper expression to the demand for equity and "climate justice"... [heads of government] will need to feel the heat of a worldwide people's movement breathing on their necks. There's no other way. The countdown to 2015 has begun.
>
> (Jacobs 2012)

This book contributes to this discussion by considering the role that civil society organizations play in global climate politics. I make three contributions that are relevant to scholars, policy-makers, and activists. First, I have examined how the network of actors mobilizing on climate change has evolved over time. In Chapter 2 I demonstrated that while this network was small and cohesive for most of its history, it became substantially larger and more diverse in advance of the Copenhagen Summit. The network fragmented under this pressure, becoming much less cohesive than it once was. This fragmentation resulted in decreased communication and coordination of strategies among groups working at the Copenhagen Summit. The central argument is that the structure of networks influences the way that they perform.

Second, this book has explored how organizations choose their strategies when they sponsor collective action on climate change. In Chapter 3, I considered why some organizations chose to use protest strategies in Copenhagen while others did not. I examined this question using quantitative evidence, and I found that organizations tend to adopt protest strategies when their partners have already done so. Drawing on qualitative evidence in Chapters 4 and 5, I found that organizations harmonize their tactics with their peers due to information sharing, resource pooling, and social influence. The main theme of these chapters is that relationships between organizations have a large impact on tactical choices.

Third, I considered how civil society mobilization influences the trajectory of global climate change politics. I found that organizations in the divided network developed different strategic approaches. Many groups adopted contentious tactics, prompting the UNFCCC to become more restrictive in its dealings with civil society. A subset of groups also began to employ a climate justice frame, stimulating changes in the language with which states, the media, and other civil society organizations now discuss climate change issues. In Chapter 6 I demonstrated that the strategies employed by civil society groups influence global climate politics, even if this engagement sometimes produces unexpected consequences.

This conclusion will not extensively summarize my findings on these topics. Instead, I will reflect on my study and tackle three broader questions. First, what does my examination of this case tell us about cooperation between civil society groups more generally? Second, what are the implications for global climate change governance? Third, what does the future hold for the transnational climate change movement?

UNPACKING TRANSNATIONAL ADVOCACY NETWORKS

This book examines an important transnational advocacy network. My approach treats such networks as relational structures. I describe the character and functioning of these networks by employing empirical network analysis. My work shows that organizations working in this sphere are embedded in networks of communication and coordination with other groups that share broadly similar values and principles (Keck and Sikkink 1998). But I also demonstrate that they often employ different strategies in pursuit of their objectives. The strategic choices of individual organizations are both enabled and constrained by their embeddedness in broader networks.

The network I study contains highly diverse groups and is marked by significant divisions between actors. Scholars have traditionally paid less attention to divided networks than to their more consensual cousins (but see Bob 2012; Hertel 2006; Johnson 1999; Maney 2001; Nelson 2002; Smith 2008). I argue that this focus has come at the expense of theoretical precision. We need to better theorize and investigate the relationship between network structure and collective outcomes if we are to understand how and when civil society groups become influential (see also Sikkink 2009; Murdie 2014; Hafner-Burton, Kahler, and Montgomery 2009).

This book takes a first step in this direction by examining a divided network in detail in Chapter 2. But there are many remaining questions that are best answered with comparative work. Do network divisions always translate into decreased performance? Is the strategy of "speaking with one voice" a sound approach? Under what conditions can different tactics complement rather than compete with one another? Gathering comparable data about other network structures and outcomes would be useful for establishing the analytical purchase of my approach and explaining the variability in civil society influence across issue areas.

Acknowledging the diversity and fault lines within global civil society gives us a much more accurate picture of this realm of politics. Admittedly, it also complicates studies about the influence of these actors. My study makes it clear that we cannot simply study civil society participation in the UNFCCC as if the institution were the target of a single coordinated campaign. To borrow a metaphor from Sidney Tarrow (2005b), the UNFCCC functions more like a coral reef that attracts and supports a diverse ecosystem of groups. These groups pursue different strategies and demands. The cumulative effect of their advocacy has results above and beyond their individual actions.

This is a complicated picture, but one that likely describes other issue areas as well. How do we measure influence in such a context? My study focuses on two strategic innovations introduced by civil society actors and traces their implications in global climate politics. This process tracing approach has the advantage of allowing me to observe intended and unintended outcomes, but it is necessarily limited: not only am I unable to trace the implications of all of the strategic choices made in this context; I am also limited to considering those strategies that are relatively discrete and have easily observable implications. But my work also convinces me that developing methods to measure influence in these kinds of complex settings will constitute an important challenge for future research.

This book views global civil society as a complicated and often turbulent sphere of social relations. This view contrasts with earlier scholarship which tended to emphasize its cohesive nature (e.g. Florini 2005, 134; Wapner 1995, 261). My work suggests that the extent of cohesion among actors is highly variable. Like other skeptics of global civil society (Friedman, Hochstetler, and Clark 2005; Stroup 2012; Tarrow 2005b), I find that climate groups are divided in terms of their preferred tactics, substantive understandings, and frames. This does not mean that these divisions are permanent: in fact, I do see recent signs of convergence in the network I study. But my case demonstrates that the cohesion of civil society actors needs to be an empirical question, not a matter of assumption.

Social network analysis holds particular promise because it allows us to measure the extent of cohesion among actors and compare organizational populations across issue areas and over time. It can also be used to identify the source of cleavages between actors. For example, the network I analyze in this book is divided between traditional environmental NGOs and those organizations originating in the global justice movement (Hadden 2014). The analysis reveals that this cleavage is not simply reducible to a north–south divide, echoing the assessment of other recent scholarship (Doherty and Doyle 2013; Bulow 2010). This type of cleavage is familiar to those who study the World Social Forum and the politics of international financial institutions (Smith et al. 2007) and is increasingly important to those who study international environmental politics as well. This kind of analysis is much needed, as understanding the issues that divide groups helps us to better appreciate the sources of conflict between groups and may point to useful strategies for promoting future coordination.

IMPLICATIONS FOR GLOBAL CLIMATE GOVERNANCE

This book also examines the variety of ways in which civil society organizations participate in global climate governance. Both scholars and policy makers have traditionally been optimistic about the beneficial consequences of civil society involvement in global governance. Scholars emphasize that civil society participation strengthens problem-solving and increases the legitimacy of governance arrangements (Dryzek 2000, 130; Florini 2000; Higgott et al. 2000; Lipschutz 1992; Princen and Finger 1994; Reinicke 2000; Scholte and Schnabel 2002; Willetts 1996; Young

2000, 178). Policy makers often design institutions to be open to civil society groups with these benefits in mind (UNFCCC 1992; UNFCCC 2009).

But my observation of recent meetings suggests that there is a growing skepticism – originating both from within the NGO community and from states themselves – regarding the value of civil society groups' formal participation in climate governance around the UNFCCC process. Civil society groups increasingly complain that opportunities for influence have become virtually nonexistent within the UNFCCC, causing participants to fear that their continued involvement may legitimize a process that has disregarded their input. And some state delegates complain (off the record) that civil society groups distract from the serious work of the negotiations, generating additional transaction costs in an already complicated process (see also Matthews 1997).

How can we maximize the benefits of civil society participation in global climate governance? I argue that we need to take into account civil society's growing size and diversity in reimagining its role. Change is needed on two fronts. First, we need forums that can provide broader access and more deliberative opportunities for a wider range of actors. As Victor and Keohane (2010) have noted, the UNFCCC is only one part of a larger regime complex for the governance of climate change. As the climate problem is inherently beyond the scope of any one set of actors, the continued use of different venues and experiments for designing solutions and seeking input should serve to enhance the process of governing the climate (Ostrom 1990). For example, international forums like the World People's Conference on Climate Change in Bolivia and the Rio +20 People's Summit may become important venues for deliberation for social movement organizations. More technical venues, like the various subsidiary groups and financial mechanisms, may offer better opportunities for participation for other groups. Linking these venues will create opportunities for learning and knowledge spillover in this sphere. And a less exclusive focus on participation in the UNFCCC should decrease the mounting pressure on this institution and may provide more meaningful opportunities for participation in global climate governance to a wider range of actors.

Second, civil society actors urgently need deeper engagement in existing institutions. As part of this process, the UNFCCC should carefully reconsider its rules and procedures for facilitating civil society participation. I document in Chapter 6 how this institution has become more restrictive in its dealings with civil society since Copenhagen. If this policy is intended to curtail protest and confrontational activism, it is likely to be counterproductive: increased policing, combined with diminished opportunities to provide input and comment into the work of the negotiations, is likely to drive groups further outside the negotiating process. If the reduction of opportunities for participation results in decreased civil society involvement, this may ultimately weaken the institution's popular legitimacy and detract from implementation of any eventual agreement (Bernauer and Gampfer 2013, 439).

From this perspective, it is in the UNFCCC's best interest to develop a mutually satisfactory system of civil society engagement before 2015. The UNFCCC has in the past attempted to expand participation to the largest number of participants as possible. This is becoming untenable. While unpopular, limits on the total number of participants are virtually inevitable for future meetings. Such restrictions can be made more palatable by developing equitable and transparent procedures to determine who gets access and why. But I suggest that future reform must also focus on improving the quality of participation for those who do secure access. For the benefits of civil society participation to be maximized, transparency within the UNFCCC will need to increase. Civil society groups need de facto access to most documents and meetings in order to bring their diverse knowledge to the table, and they need clear rules regarding the policies and penalties associated with protest actions in order to make decisions about how best to channel their activism. I suggest that focusing on these two areas of reform, in combination with opening up broader spaces for deliberation and experimentation outside the negotiations themselves, will offer the best chance of securing meaningful civil society engagement in global climate governance.

THE FUTURE OF THE TRANSNATIONAL CLIMATE MOVEMENT

This book opens the door to a view of the internal relations of civil society as a distinct sphere of governance. Networks are not power free: they enable and constrain the choices of those actors working within them. As Scholte (2002, 298) points out, "civil society associations that deal with global governance issues can in some cases actively constrain discussion and suppress dissent." In this case, as in others, some groups dominate agenda-setting and policy-setting (Carpenter 2014; Dalton and Rohrschneider 2002;). Actors wield influence over one another, changing the overall strategic composition of the organizational population. Studying these intranetwork dynamics expands our understanding of how power operates within this fascinating and unexplored layer of social organization.

This book has documented two different models for how civil society might govern itself internally. Chapter 4 considered the Climate Action Network, one of the world's largest civil society coalitions, which has been in continuous operation for more than twenty-five years. Chapter 5 explored the emergence of a more decentralized coalition of groups working under the banner of the climate justice movement. The analysis showed that the CAN model is much more formalized and contractual, whereas the climate justice model tends to be more fluid and self-reinforcing. The CAN approach generates buy-in from large organizations, but then must necessarily privilege the positions of these groups in its decision making. The climate justice approach is more consensual and horizontal, but requires enormous amounts of time and commitment to function effectively. Both models have significant challenges and limitations. But they both also represent generally successful attempts to mitigate the coordination problems that exist among groups working in this sphere.

Whether ultimately these two different coalition structures can learn to work together or to develop a new hybrid mode of internal governance will be fascinating to observe.

What does the future hold for the transnational climate change movement? This book documents how divisions emerged in the climate network at a critical moment – but there are reasons to believe these divisions may be bridged. I write this book at a time in which many civil society groups are regrouping for the next round of negotiations. As the Climate Action Network stated in a call for participation during its anniversary retreat:

> After the Copenhagen Climate Summit in 2009, the climate movement lost momentum, and until now it has not regained that lost ground. But now, signs of a new uprising of the movement are taking shape. After several years of reflection and reassessment, civil society and other stakeholders have started to raise urgency around climate change again, bringing new energy and a different rhetoric to the climate debate.
>
> (Climate Action Network 2014)

There are three main avenues by which the movement has evolved since Copenhagen. The first development has been the recognition of decreased opportunities for participation and activism around the UNFCCC. These restrictions amount to a significant closure of political opportunities, as lamented by many groups. As one explained:

> After Copenhagen, security has been particularly by the book. The problem is, we never knew where the line was to begin with. The rules have never been that clear. People were getting kicked out without even knowing what they had done wrong. So it was very upsetting and really turned some people off.
>
> (Interview, Climate Action Network 2011)

The perception that opportunities for participation in the UNFCCC are limited may drive groups to change their tactics. This could have two potential consequences. We may see large-scale protest become the norm at future high-profile conferences. If this prediction is correct, the tentative civil society walkout in Warsaw may presage a more contentious climate movement once the UNFCCC heads to Paris for its 2015 meeting. It may also lead to more tactical similarity between the two sides of the network in the next few years, offering more opportunities for coordination and joint actions.

We may also see a shift in the targets favored by the movement. Climate activists increasingly perceive the UNFCCC as less central to the climate debate and have been targeting corporations, national governments, and individuals to a greater extent. As one campaigner explained it: "I think Doha was a real low point in terms of engaging with the UNFCCC . . . there were some clear limitations there. So it seemed clear that we need to scale down our activities there and work more on this movement building" (Interview, Oxfam International, 2013). The idea that the UNFCCC will not produce an acceptable climate change agreement – once considered a radical position even within the climate justice movement – now seems to be a fairly mainstream view. As an activist explained it to me, "it's time for us to get over our Stockholm Syndrome" (Interview, Climate Justice Now, 2013). Activists may be moving on to other arenas of struggle on climate change.

Many activists have decided to focus more on domestic targets in the post-Copenhagen period. Scholars know that powerful transnational movements have deep roots in domestic politics (Bülow 2010; Tarrow 2005b); thus, building stronger domestic ties may allow the movement more flexibility when transnational political opportunities are closed off. It may also expand the resource base for future transnational action. The North American struggle against the Keystone pipeline is a good example of this kind of shift in targets. But this transformation does not amount to an abandonment of international activism. Many climate organizations have also been highly mobilized around the UN post-2015 Sustainable Development agenda, working to integrate climate concerns into broader discussions about sustainable development. And even those groups that have shifted to primarily domestic work have retained their international ties, making the potential for transnational mobilization an ever-present possibility.

Third, much of the current energy in the climate change movement – even among mainstream environmental NGOs – centers on making normative contestation the basis of broader movement building. As one campaigner explained to me, the convergence on the climate justice frame documented in Chapter 6 is central to this strategy:

> I think what happened in Copenhagen was that a lot of NGOs – northern NGOs, us included – were working for a long time with a frame that was very technical and demotivating for a lot of people. And it was really based on a theory of change that "if we change our governments, we can change the system." Climate justice is much bigger than that. Climate justice helps us build the movement.
>
> (Interview, Friends of the Earth International, 2013)

Another explained that the goal is "to make coal the new cigarettes" and to debate the issue on a moral level, rather than by forefronting science (Interview, 350.org, 2013). Scholars have previously documented how normative contestation has been a key strategy in many successful environmental campaigns, chief among them the anti-whaling movement (Epstein 2008; Peterson 1992). The climate movement's ability to leverage this form of power will be an exciting issue to examine and a key strategy going forward.

The climate movement certainly faces a number of challenges. Central to the theme of this book is one of the movement's key questions: how can climate change organizations best coordinate, given the incredible growth in their numbers and diversity? As Smith's (2008a, 233) study of the global justice movement shows, movements are strongest when they both support diversity in positions and are able to form cohesive alliances (see also Khagram 2004). My study makes it clear that climate change organizations would benefit from more attention to their internal network governance. There is a critical need to invest in dialogue and brokerage to achieve desired ends. This does not mean that groups need to take the same action; the potential to trigger a radical flank effect remains open if groups can meaningfully coordinate tactics and goals (Haines 1984; Gupta 2003). But more discussion and trust building, in order to bridge existing enclaves within the network, is critical if the full power of civil society is to be realized. Increasing size and diversity pose a challenge to these objectives – but not one that cannot be overcome.

This book argues that civil society organizations play an important role in global climate politics. I suggest that the lessons from Copenhagen concern relations within the movement as much as the strategies and tactics that it might employ. The "power in movement" comes from the strength of its internal networks. Investigating these networks should be a central enterprise for those who seek to understand why they succeed or fail – and investing in these networks should be a central goal for activists seeking to influence climate policy in the years to come.

Main Abbreviations Used

ALBA	Bolivarian Alliance for the Peoples of Our America
CAN	Climate Action Network
CJA	Climate Justice Action
CJN	Climate Justice Now!
CO_2	Carbon Dioxide
COP	Conference of the Parties
ENB	Earth Negotiations Bulletin
ENGO	Environmental Nongovernmental Organization
ESF	European Social Forum
EU	European Union
FOE	Friends of the Earth
FOE-I	Friends of the Earth International
GCCA	Global Campaign for Climate Action
GHG	Greenhouse Gas
IMF	International Monetary Fund
IPCC	Intergovernmental Panel on Climate Change
LCA	Long-term Cooperative Action
NGO	Nongovernmental Organization
NTAC	Never Trust a COP
SBI	Subsidiary Body on Implementation
T&E	Transport and Environment
UK	United Kingdom

UNFCCC United Nations Framework Convention on Climate
        Change
WTO   World Trade Organization
WWF   World Wildlife Fund

Methods Appendix

QUANTITATIVE DATA

Chapters 3 and 6 rely on original quantitative data. This section describes the research procedures that led to the collection of data on organizations, their forms of action, network ties, and attributes discussed in Chapter 3. It also describes the protest event analysis and coding of state speeches presented in Chapter 6.

Event Data

To gather systematic data on collective action on climate change, I conducted a large-scale protest event analysis. Newspaper reports are frequently used in the tradition of protest event analysis to gather systematic information about the volume, timing, and characteristics of contentious collective action (Koopmans and Rucht 2002). I followed this approach by conducting an electronic search across a variety of media outlets to identify relevant events.

For this portion of my study, I decided to limit myself to an analysis of transnational collective action in the European Union (see Chapter 3). Therefore, I searched using two separate sets of terms: (1) (EU or EC or Europe*) AND (climate change or global warming) and (2) (climate change or global warming) AND (protest* or strike* or demonstration*), for the dates January 1, 2008 to December 31, 2009. The second search was added to capture transnational collective action on climate change within the European Union that does not target the EU. From the returned items, I selected those that involved any sort of collective action. In both searches, articles had to be sorted by hand according to two criteria: (1) the action had to be a transnational collective action on climate change that took place in the European Union, and (2) it had to involve a civil society organization. An action qualified as a transnational collective action if it targeted an international institution or if it involved mobilization in more than one country.

I use the term "civil society" loosely to denote a "self-organized citizenry" that includes social movements, trade unions, and nongovernmental organizations but excludes state or corporate actors (Edwards, Foley, and Diani 2001; Emirbayer and Sheller 1999). For the purposes of my analysis, this includes organizations that make "public interest claims" and "pursue social change" (Andrews and Edwards 2004, 486). Though I require such organizations to be sufficiently institutionalized to publicly sponsor collective actions, I do not make an a priori distinction between NGOs and social movements.

These search terms returned 11,588 hits for the years 2008–9, from which 371 (3.2 percent) involved a relevant collective action, resulting in the selection of 371 reports of 262 unique events. These searches were conducted across the Reuters newswire (general and EU); the *Financial Times*; and the wire services stories of the Associated Press Worldstream, the Deutsche Presse-Agentur, and Agence France Presse. In addition, I searched the online archive of Euractiv.com for stories about "climate change" or "global warming" and read the entirety of the Indymedia Climate and the Rising Tide news for the same time period.

Once I had selected the relevant event sample, these events were coded dichotomously as being either contentious or conventional. I also coded if the event targeted either the UN or the EU. Table A.1 details this procedure.

TABLE A.1. *Code Book for Event Data*

Code Name	Description
Contentious	Includes public assembly, march, demonstration (legal and nonviolent), vigil/picket, illegal demonstration (if nonviolent), boycott, strike, self-mutilation (e.g., hunger strike, suicide), blockade, occupation, disturbance of meetings, symbolic confrontation (e.g., farmers dumping animal dung in front of a government building), threats (e.g., bomb threat), symbolic violence (e.g., burning puppets or flags, throwing eggs or paint), limited destruction of property (e.g., breaking windows), sabotage, violent demonstration (violence initiated by protesters), arson and bomb attacks, and other severe destruction of property, arson and bomb attacks against people (incl. inhabited buildings), physical violence against people (fights, brawls, etc.). Each day of protest is counted as a separate event.
Conventional	Includes press conference/release, public speech, (public) letter, newspaper article, book, research report, leaflet, etc., presentation of survey/poll result, publicity campaign (incl. advertising), conferences/meetings/assemblies, other "petitioning," petition/signature collection, letter campaigning. Interviews with civil society leaders were not counted as collective actions.
EU Target	Actions taken that are addressed to the European Commission, Parliament, Council or Court of Justice.
UN Target	Actions taken that are addressed to the United Nations or affiliate (e.g., UNFCCC).

My coding follows the approach outlined in the "Codebook for the Analysis of Political Mobilisation and Communication in European Public Spheres" developed by Ruud Koopmans (2002), as well as the "Interview Questionnaire for Interviews with Collective Actors in Claims-making and Political Mobilization" used for the DEMOS project (Kriesi 2007).

Scholars working with newspaper data point to two potential sources of bias: selection bias and description bias (Earl et al. 2004). Because I code only "hard facts" about the action (e.g., place, time, and form), I expect description bias to be less of an issue for my study (Koopmans and Rucht 2002, 2237). I rely on additional research procedures to identify sponsors (see later discussion on network data), also limiting potential description biases associated with press sources reporting only the most established actors.

Selection bias is a more serious issue for this study. In my data collection procedures, I tried to be as comprehensive as possible by (1) combining a number of different sources, (2) not using indexes or "headline only" searches, and (3) not sampling from press sources. But I still had two potential concerns about the data. First, conducting the search in English might increase the number of events in my sample that took place in the United Kingdom. I tried to correct for this geographical bias by including a broad selection of sources, including the Associated Press Worldstream, Agence France Press, and Deutsche Presse-Agentur databases (in translation), and the Reuters newswire (general and EU). The UK was in fact the third most common location for events in my sample (after Belgium and Denmark). But the extent to which this reflects a bias in the data collection is difficult to ascertain, because the UK is also an important country for innovative climate change organizing.

Second, I was concerned that my use of alternative media might introduce a bias in favor of contentious events. However, after evaluating the press sources, I decided that the extent of this bias was probably not extensive. For example, a comparison between my database and the Reuters newswire used in the Imig and Tarrow (2001) and Uba and Uggla (2011) studies showed little difference in the percentage of contentious events reported.

Network Data

From the returned news items, I was able to create a database of reported events. I then conducted document research on each event, seeking out copies of joint press releases, lists of organizational event sponsors, and other primary source material. These documents were obtained via two routes. If specific organizations were identified, I sought out copies of the relevant documents on their websites. When news reports were not specific enough, I conducted a search of different email listservs to which I was subscribed from 2007 to 2009.

From this document analysis, I was able to gather more complete information about which organizations sponsored which collective actions. This stage of data collection was essential to gathering accurate network data, as I found that newspaper articles were often inaccurate or incomplete in their reporting of organizations. This affiliation between organizations and events was then recorded in matrix format, resulting in a two-mode network.

Organizational Data

In addition to knowing the organizational sponsors of particular events, my statistical analysis required knowing key attributes of these organizations. To gather this information, I systematically coded the websites of organizations that appeared in my sample. In most instances, this information was available publicly or through the Internet archive (www.archive.org). In a few instances, I needed to collect this information over the phone or by requesting annual reports. In addition, I gathered data about whether an organization received EU funding from institutional records of the European Commission and Parliament.

I collected data on five important organizational attributes: whether the organization had a radical ideology, whether it received EU funding, whether it had an organizational structure that accommodates individual members, the number of full-time staff it employed in 2009, and its age in 2009. Table A.2 details this coding procedure.

These data were pooled to create a dataset of organizations and their ties, as well as their attributes and the kinds of events they sponsor. Table A.3 summarizes the variables used in the analysis in Chapter 3.

TABLE A.2. *Organizational Attribute Code Book*

Variable	Description
Radical Ideology	Coded as present if the organization has anticapitalist or antisystemic references on its website.
Receives EU Funding	Coded as present if the organization appears in the register of the European Commission and the European Parliament as receiving funding for the year 2009.
Has Individual Members	Coded as present if the organization has content on its websites or in its charter that permits individuals to join as members.
Number of Full-Time Staff	Coded as the number of full-time staff employed by the organization in 2009.
Age	Coded as the number of years the organization had been in operation in 2009.

TABLE A.3. *Summary Statistics for Variables in Chapter 3*

Variable	Mean	SD	Description
Number of Contentious Ties in 2008	1.77	2.16	Total number of ties an organization had with contentious organizations (those using >50% contentious actions) in 2008.
Number of Contentious Actions in 2008	1.03	2.01	Total number of contentious collective actions the organization sponsored in 2008.
Number of Contentious Events Reported in the Previous Month	8.63	6.26	Total number of contentious events reported in press sample in the previous month/1000.
Radical Ideology	.155	.362	Yes=1. Coded for the presence of anticapitalist or antisystemic references on the organization's website.

TABLE A.3. (*cont.*)

Variable	Mean	SD	Description
Receives EU Funding	0.34	0.47	Yes=1. Based on coding of whether the organization appears in the register of the European Commission and the European Parliament as receiving funding for the year 2009.
Has Individual Members	0.57	0.50	Yes=1. Based on the coding of websites and organizational charters to see if the organization permits individuals to join as members.
Number of Full-Time Staff	36.97	67.57	Number of full-time staff employed by the organization in 2009.
Age	21.64	12.87	Age of the organization in 2009 (i.e., 2009 – founding date).

Other Quantitative Data

For Chapter 6, I conducted an additional protest event analysis to gather data on the relative frequency of contentious events on climate change around the UNFCCC from 2005 to 2013. I searched the LexisNexis database for all articles that met the search terms "(climate change or global warming) AND (UN or United Nations) AND (protest* or march* or demonstration*)" for the two-week time period of each of the COPs held from 2005 to 2013. Each returned article was then hand-coded to determine if it contained a relevant contentious action, as defined by the codebook mentioned earlier. In addition, I coded an alternate source – the *Earth Negotiations Bulletin* – for mentions of contentious collective action on climate change. For this task, each daily bulletin for every COP was read and coded by hand for the presence of contentious collective action.

I also conducted coding of state speeches at the UNFCCC on climate change. These speeches are given at the joint high-level segment of every conference. Typically, every state that is a party to the UNFCCC will speak for approximately eight minutes, outlining its position on climate change. These speeches exist on the UNFCCC website in either video or PDF format. For this analysis, research assistants listened to every state speech and coded each for the presence of the terms "climate justice," "justice," or "equity" in the years 2005, 2007, 2009, 2011, and 2013. Research assistants also noted when states discussed the principles of justice using other terms, including "fairness" and "common but differentiated responsibilities."

Finally, I coded each article from approximately 100 issues of the CAN newsletter *ECO* from 2005 to 2013. Each *ECO* article was coded in Atlas.ti as employing a justice/equity framing, a scientific framing, or both. To identify a justice/equity framing, I coded direct references in the text to "justice" and "equity," as well as associated concepts such as "fairness" and "common but differentiated responsibilities." To identify a scientific framing, I coded direct references to scientific evidence (e.g., the IPCC), scientific targets (e.g., 350 ppm), or scientific urgency.

QUALITATIVE DATA

In Chapters 2, 4, and 5, I relied on extensive original qualitative data. This section describes the procedures by which I collected interviews, documents, and observations for this study.

Interviews

I conducted more than ninety interviews with approximately seventy civil society organizations working on climate change. The bulk of the interviews were conducted between September 2008 and December 2009, although I also conducted interviews in summer 2007 and after 2009, especially around subsequent

COPs. Drawing on my analysis of protest events from Chapter 3 as a preliminary roster, I randomly selected organizations from different portions of the civil society network (stratified by centrality score) to approach for interviews. In a second phase, I sampled those organizations that occupied key network positions or that were mentioned by respondents as especially influential. For interviews after 2009, I approached those actors that I knew to be central in the network and who were good informants. In both phases, my response rate to interview requests was more than 90 percent. Table A.4 contains a complete list of interviews.

Once I had identified my sample, I conducted semistructured interviews with representatives of the organizations. Typically, this was either the head of the organization, the person in charge of the climate campaign, or a longtime activist familiar with the climate work of the organization. Where organizations were decentralized in their decision making or had experienced a recent turnover in staff, I sometimes conducted more than one interview with the same organization.

The interviews involved both structured questions (how many staff members does your organization have) and more open-ended questions (describe the actions your organization is involved in). Interviews were conducted in both English and French, and ranged between thirty minutes and three hours, but typically lasted about one hour. Interviews were generally recorded and transcribed, except when participants requested that they not be, as was more typical in contentious groups (especially those involved in illegal actions). In those cases, I took notes by hand and wrote up a transcript to the best of my recollection immediately afterward. Participants in the interviews were given a guarantee that their identity would be kept confidential but were informed that I intended to associate their responses with the name of their organization.

I coded the interview transcripts using the software program Atlas.ti. In my coding, I looked for patterns in the ways that organizations described their decision making about tactics. I had previously identified mechanisms in the scholarly literature that I expected might operate within these organizations, but I also

TABLE A.4. *List of Organizational Interviews Conducted by the Author*

Organization Name	Number of Interviews	Dates
350.org	2	December 2010; November 2013
Attac France	1	October 2009
Avaaz.org	1	January 2010
Avenir Climat	1	October 2009
Camp for Climate Action UK	1	January 2009
Climate Action Network Europe	3	July 2007; December 2008; October 2009
Climate Action Network International	6	December 2008; December 2009; December 2010; December 2011; July 2012; November 2013
Climate Action Network US	2	December 2008; December 2009
Climate Camp Belgium/Netherlands	1	November 2009
Climate Camp France	1	October 2009
Climate Camp Germany	1	December 2009
Climate Camp UK	1	August 2009
Climate Justice Action	3	September 2008; March 2009; December 2009
Climate Justice Caravan	1	December 2009
Climate Justice Fast	1	December 2009
Climate Justice Now!	5	December 2008; December 2009; August 2010; December 2010; November 2013
Danish 92 Group	1	December 2009
Dialogo Climatico	1	December 2010
Earth First!	2	September 2008; November 2009

TABLE A.4. (*cont.*)

Organization Name	Number of Interviews	Dates
Ecologistas en Accion	1	December 2009
Espaces Karl Marx	1	October 2009
European Environmental Bureau	1	September 2009
European Youth for Action	1	November 2009
Friends of the Earth Brazil	1	December 2010
Friends of the Earth Denmark	2	November 2009; December 2010
Friends of the Earth Europe	2	October 2008; November 2009
Friends of the Earth France	1	October 2008
Friends of the Earth Germany	1	January 2010
Friends of the Earth International	4	September 2008; March 2009; December 2009; November 2013
Friends of the Earth Latin America	1	December 2010
Friends of the Earth Sweden	1	December 2009
Friends of the Earth UK	1	September 2011
Friends of the Earth Youth	1	September 2008
Global Campaign Against Climate Change	2	December 2008; December 2009
Global Campaign for Climate Action	2	August 2009
Global Forests Coalition	1	December 2010

Table A.4. (*cont.*)

Organization Name	Number of Interviews	Dates
Global Justice Ecology Project	1	September 2008
Greenpeace European Unit	3	July 2007; March 2009; October 2009
Greenpeace International	2	December 2008; January 2010
Greenpeace Italy	1	December 2009
Greenpeace Nordic	1	December 2009
Greenpeace UK	1	August 2009
Grupo de Reflexion Rural	1	December 2012
Indigenous Environmental Network	1	December 2010
Initiatives Pour un Autre Monde	1	October 2009
Jubilee Debt Campaign	1	December 2010
Klima Allianz	1	December 2009
Klimaforum [Denmark]	2	December 2009
Klimaforum [Mexico]	2	December 2010
Klimataktion Sweden	1	September 2008
Klimax	3	September 2008; December 2009
La Via Campesina	2	December 2009; December 2010
La Via Campesina Europe	1	November 2009
Oxfam GB	1	August 2009
Oxfam International	3	May 2009; November 2009; November 2013
People and Planet	1	August 2009
Peoples' Global Action	1	December 2009

TABLE A.4. (*cont.*)

Organization Name	Number of Interviews	Dates
Plane Stupid	1	August 2009
Polish Ecological Club	1	December 2008
Reseau d'Action Climat France	1	October 2009
Rising Tide	2	January 2010
Rising Tide Mexico	1	December 2010
Rising Tide UK	1	August 2009
The Transnational Institute	1	November 2009
Transport and Environment Europe	1	November 2009
Wetlands International	1	December 2009
World Development Movement	1	December 2010
WWF European Policy Office	2	July 2007; October 2009
WWF International	1	October 2009
WWF UK	1	August 2009

coded inductively, keeping an eye open for unexpected processes that might emerge from the data. This coding allowed me to discuss the relative frequency of different processes in organizational decision making, as well as to draw on illustrative examples of each mechanism.

Observation, Emails, and Documents

In addition to the interviews, I collected three other types of qualitative data. First, I attended approximately 200 hours of intraorganizational and coalitional meetings during the time period of this study. I witnessed most of the events described in this book. Table A.5 describes those that were most important

TABLE A.5. *Selected Organizational Observations Conducted by the Author*

Organization Name	Activity Type	Date
Climate Justice Action	Strategy Meeting	September 2008
European Social Forum Radical Assembly	Information and Outreach Meeting	September 2008
CAN International	Daily Strategy and Coordination Sessions	December 2008
Climate Justice Action	Outreach and Strategy Meeting	December 2008
Campaign Against Climate Change	Demonstration and March	December 2008
Climate Camp UK	London Climate Camp, Copenhagen Strategy Meeting	August 2009
Attac France	Climate Information Meeting and Debate	November 2009
Dutch Climate Justice Action	Information Meeting	November 2009
Climate Justice Caravan	Outreach Tour	December 2009
CAN International	Daily Strategy and Coordination Sessions	December 2009
Climate Justice Now!	Daily Strategy and Coordination Sessions	December 2009
Climate Justice Action	Strategy, Action, Evaluation, and Spokes Council Meetings	December 2009
Friends of the Earth International	Human Flood Demonstration	December 2009
Global Campaign for Climate Action	Demonstration and March	December 2009
KlimaForum	Alternative Summit and Workshops	December 2009

TABLE A.5. (*cont.*)

Organization Name	Activity Type	Date
Climate Justice Action–Climate Justice Now!	Reclaim Power! and Peoples Assembly	December 2009
Climate Justice Action	Prisoners Solidarity Demonstration	December 2009
CAN International	Daily Strategy and Coordination Sessions	December 2010
Climate Justice Now!	Daily Strategy and Coordination Sessions	December 2010
Klimaforum/Dialogo Climatico	Alternative Summit and Workshops	December 2010
La Via Campesina	Encampment and March	December 2010
Global Campaign for Climate Action	Demonstration and March	December 2010

for developing my analysis. I wrote up my observations of these meetings as field notes. These observations have especially informed Chapters 4 and 5.

In particular, I attended many of the meetings of Climate Justice Action and the Climate Action Network from September 2008 to December 2009. In the case of CAN, I was given access to the coalition and its staff but was asked to respect the confidentiality agreement in place within the coalition. My observations with CAN particularly informed my understanding of how the coalition operates within the UNFCCC political processes. Attending these meetings also introduced me to the important individuals and organizations working in this sphere of advocacy. But I do not report directly on these meetings unless they have been discussed in on-the-record interviews. In the case of Climate Justice Action, I was allowed to observe and write about the coalition provided that I did something useful (usually washing dishes or cooking) and did not identify people at meetings by their name or organization. Because of my agreement with participants, I am able to discuss the internal functioning of CJA in much more detail than that of CAN.

I was also subscribed to a number of internal email list servs during this time period. Specifically, I was subscribed to the private internal listservs of CAN Europe and CAN International, as well as to the public lists of CJA and CJN. During the time period of this study, I collected more than 10,000 emails through these channels, which kept me exceptionally well informed about the political process and the workings of these coalitions. As all these emails are confidential, I do not discuss their contents except when they exist in the public sphere or have been discussed in on-the-record interviews.

Finally, I gathered hundreds of coalitional and organizational documents during my fieldwork. I particularly sought out organizational documents that described internal work procedures or decision making processes. I employ these documents to better inform my case studies and as a check on the validity of my interview data.

References

350.org. 2009. "International Day of Climate Action." Available online at: http://350.org/en/node/18474. Retrieved May 10, 2014.

ALBA. 2009. "Joint Statement on the Outcome of COP 15." Available online at: http://venezuelanalysis.com/analysis/5038. Retrieved May 10, 2014.

Alcock, Frank. 2008. "Conflict and Coalitions Within and Across the ENGO Community." *Global Environmental Politics* 8 (4): 66–91.

Andrews, Kenneth T., and Bob Edwards. 2004. "Advocacy Organizations in the U.S. Political Process." *Annual Review of Sociology* 30 (4): 479–506.

Ansell, Christopher. 2003. "Community Embeddedness and Collaborative Governance in the San Francisco Bay Area Environmental Movement." In *Social Movements and Networks*, edited by Mario Diani and Doug McAdam. Oxford: Oxford University Press, 123–144.

Avant, Deborah, Martha Finnemore, and Susan K. Sell. 2010. *Who Governs the Globe?* New York: Cambridge University Press.

Bandy, Joe, and Jackie Smith. 2005. *Coalitions Across Borders: Transnational Protest and the Neoliberal Order*. Lanham, MD: Rowman & Littlefield.

Barakso, Maryann. 2010. "Brand Identity and the Tactical Repertoires of Advocacy Organizations." In *Advocacy Organizations and Collective Action*, edited by Aseem Prakash and Mary Kay Gugerty. New York: Cambridge University Press, 155–176.

Barrett, Scott. 2009. "Rethinking Global Climate Change Governance." *Economics: The Open-Access, Open-Assessment E-Journal*. Available online at: www.economics-ejournal.org/economics/journalarticles/2009-5. Retrieved May 23, 2014.

Baumgartner, Frank, and Beth Leech. 1998. *Basic Interests*. Princeton, NJ: Princeton University Press.

BBC News. 2009. "Copenhagen Deal Reactions in Quotes." *BBC Online*. Available online at: http://news.bbc.co.uk/2/hi/science/nature/8421910.stm. Retrieved May 10, 2014.

Bell, Ruth Greenspan, and Barry Blechman. 2014. "Opinion: Time to Look Beyond the UN Climate Negotations." *The Daily Climate*. Available online at: www.dailyclimate.org/tdc-newsroom/2014/02/nuclear-proliferation-climate-talks. Retrieved May 23, 2014.

Bennett, Lance. 2004. "Global Media and Politics: Transnational Communication Regimes and Civic Cultures." *Annual Review of Political Science* 7: 125–148.

Bennett, Lance and Alexandra Segerberg. 2013. *The Logic of Connective Action: Digital Media and the Personalization of Contentious Politics*. New York: Cambridge University Press.

Bernauer, Thomas, and Robert Gampfer. 2013. "Effects of Civil Society Involvement on Popular Legitimacy of Global Environmental Governance." *Global Environmental Change* 23 (2): 439–449.

Betsill, Michele. 2000. *Greens in the Greenhouse: Environmental NGOs, Norms and the Politics Global Climate Change*. Doctoral dissertation, University of Colorado Department of Political Science.

    2006. "Transnational Actors in International Environmental Politics." In *Palgrave Advances in International Environmental Politics*, edited by Michele M. Betsill, Kathryn Hochstetler, and Dimitris Stevis. New York: Palgrave, 172–202.

Betsill, Michele M., and Elisabeth Corell. 2001. "A Comparative Look at NGO Influence in International Environmental Negotiations: Desertification and Climate Change." *Global Environmental Politics* 1 (4): 86–107.

Bob, Clifford. 2005. *The Marketing of Rebellion: Insurgents, Media, and International Activism*. New York: Cambridge University Press.

    2012. *The Global Right Wing and the Clash of World Politics*. New York: Cambridge University Press.

Bohmelt, Tobias. 2013. "A Closer Look at the Information Provision Rationale: Civil Society Participation in States' Delegations at the UNFCCC." *Review of International Organizations* 8 (1): 55–80.

Bond, Patrick. 2012. *Politics of Climate Justice*. Scottsville: University of KwaZulu-Natal Press.

Boykoff, Maxwell. 2013. "Media Coverage of Climate Change." Available online at: http://sciencepolicy.colorado.edu/media_coverage/. Retrieved May 10, 2014.

Brand, Ulrich, Nicola Bullard, Edgardo Lander, and Tadzio Mueller. 2009. "Contours of Climate Justice: Ideas for Shaping New Climate and Energy Politics." *Critical Currents*. Available online at: www. dhf.uu.se/publications/critical-currents/contours-of-climate-justice-ideas-for-shaping-new-climate-and-energy-politics/. Retrieved May 10, 2014.

Brulle, Robert J. 2000. *Agency, Democracy and Nature: The US Environmental Movement from a Critical Theory Perspective*. Cambridge, MA: MIT Press.

Bülow, Marisa Von. 2010. *Building Transnational Networks: Civil Society and the Politics of Trade in the Americas*. New York: Cambridge University Press.

Burt, Ron. 1982. *Toward a Structural Theory of Action*. New York: Academic Press.

1992. *Structural Holes: The Structure of Competition*. Cambridge, MA: Harvard University Press.

2010. *Neighbor Networks*. Oxford: Oxford University Press.

Busby, Joshua W. 2010. *Moral Movements and Foreign Policy*. Cambridge: Cambridge University Press.

Byrd, S.C. 2010. *Framing Cascades in the Climate Justice Movement*. Doctoral Dissertation, University of California Irvine, Department of Sociology.

Byrd, Scott, and Lorien Jasny. 2010. "Transnational Movement Innovation and Collaboration: An Analysis of World Social Forum Networks." *Social Movement Studies* 2 (9): 355–372.

Cable, Sherry, and Thomas Shriver. 1995. "Production and Extrapolation of Meaning in the Environmental Justice Movement." *Social Spectrum* 15 (4): 419–442.

Cabré, Miquel Muñoz. 2011. "Issue-linkages to Climate Change Measured through NGO Participation in the UNFCCC." *Global Environmental Politics* 11 (3): 10–22.

Capek, Stella M. 1993. "The 'Environmental Justice' Frame: A Conceptual Discussion and Application." *Social Problems* 40 (1): 5–24.

Carmin, JoAnn, and Deborah B. Basler. 2002. "Selecting Repertoires of Action in Environmental Movement Organizations: An Interpretive Approach." *Organization Environment* 15 (3):365–388.

Carpenter, Chad. 2001. "Business, Green Groups and the Media: The Role of Non-Governmental Organizations in the Climate Change Debate." *International Affairs* 77 (2): 313–328.

Carpenter, R. Charli. 2011. "Vetting the Advocacy Agenda: Network Centrality and the Paradox of Weapons Norms." *International Organization* 65 (1): 69–102.

Carpenter, R. Charli. 2014. *Lost Causes: Agenda Vetting in Global Issue Networks and the Shaping of Human Security*. Ithaca: Cornell University Press.

Chavez, Hugo. 2009. Transcribed from video recording of UNFCCC floor speech December 18, 2009. Available online at: http://unfccc2. meta-fusion.com/kongresse/cop15_hls/templ/play.php?id_kongresssession=4288. Retrieved May 10, 2014.

Clapp, Jennifer, and Peter Dauvergne. 2005. *Paths to a Green World: The Political Economy of the Global Environment.* Cambridge, MA: MIT Press.

Clemens, Elisabeth S., and Debra C. Minkoff. 2004. "Beyond the Iron Law: Rethinking the Place of Organizations in Social Movement Research." In *The Blackwell Companion to Social Movements*, edited by David A. Snow, Sarah Anne Soule and Hanspeter Kriesi. Malden, MA: Blackwell Publishing, 155–170.

Climate Action Network. 1996. "ECO Newsletters, COP-2." Available online at: http://web.archive.org/web/19961024000537/; http://www.igc.apc.org/climate/Eco.html. Retrieved May 14, 2014.

——— 2001. "About Us." Available online at: http://web.archive.org/web/20010308070815/; http://www.climatenetwork.org/canoffices.html. Retrieved May 14, 2014.

——— 2008. "Equity Summit Report." Available online at: www.cansea.org/wordpress/. Retrieved May 14, 2014.

——— 2009a. "ECO Newsletter, December 17, 2009." Available online at: www.climatenetwork.org/eco-newsletters?field_event_nid=260. Retrieved May 14, 2014.

——— 2009b. "Fair, Ambitious & Binding: Essentials for a Successful Climate Deal." Available online at: http://climatenetwork.org/publication/cans-fair-ambitious-binding-essentials-successful-climate-deal. Retrieved May 14, 2014.

——— 2009c. "Position Paper: The Role of International Offsets in Light of Current Annex I Emissions Reduction Targets and Climate Financing Commitments." Available online at: www.climatenetwork.org/sites/default/files/CAN_position_offsets_Nov09.pdf. Retrieved May 14, 2014.

——— 2010 "The Benefits of Public Participation." *ECO Newsletter* 16 (4): 1.

——— 2014. "CAN 25th Anniversary Celebration." Available online at: www.climatenetwork.org/event/can-25th-anniversary-celebration. Retrieved May 23, 2014.

Climate Justice Action. 2009. "March Meeting Handbook." Available online at: www.climate-justice-action.org/resources/documents/. Retrieved January 15, 2013.

Climate Justice Now! 2008. "CJN! Poznan Statement." Available online at: www.climate-justice-now.org/category/reports_and_publications/statements-and-press-releases-related-to-the-unfccc/page/4/." Retrieved February 13, 2010.

2009. "About Us." Available online at: www.climate-justice-now.org/. Retrieved February 13, 2010.

Coleman, James S. 1986. "Social Theory, Social Research, and a Theory of Action." *American Journal of Sociology* 91 (6): 1309–1335.

Cooley, Alexander, and James Ron. 2001. "The NGO Scramble." *International Security* 27 (1): 5–39.

Corn, David. 2009. "In Copenhagen, U.S. vs. China." *The Atlantic.* Available online at: www.theatlantic.com/magazine/archive/2009/12/in-copenhagen-us-vs-china/307809/. Retrieved May 23, 2014.

Cress, Daniel M., and David A. Snow. 1996. "Mobilization at the Margins: Resources, Benefactors, and the Viability of Homeless Social Movement Organizations." *American Sociological Review* 61 (6): 1098–1109.

Dalton, R.J., S. Recchia, and R. Rohrschneider. 2003. "The Environmental Movement and the Modes of Political Action." *Comparative Political Studies* 36 (7): 743–771.

Dalton, Russell J. 1994. *The Green Rainbow: Environmental Groups in Western Europe.* New Haven, CT: Yale University Press.

Davis, Gerald F., and Henrich R. Greve. 1997. "Corporate Elite Networks and Governance Changes in the 1980s." *American Journal of Sociology* 103 (1): 1–37.

Della Porta, Donatella. 2005. "Multiple Belongings, Tolerant Identities, and the Construction of 'Another Politics': Between the European Social Forum and the Local Social Fora." In *Transnational Protest and Global Activism*, edited by Donatella della Porta and Sidney Tarrow. Lanham, MD: Rowman and Littlefield, 175–202.

2007a. "The Europeanization of Protest: A Typology and Empirical Evidence." In *Debating the Democratic Legitimacy of the European Union*, edited by Beate Kohler-Koch and Berthold Rittberger. Lanham, MD: Rowman and Littlefield, 189–208.

2007b. *The Global Justice Movement: Cross-National and Transnational Perspectives.* Boulder, CO: Paradigm Publishers.

Della Porta, Donatella, and Mario Diani. 2006. *Social Movements: An Introduction.* New York: Wiley-Blackwell.

Della Porta, Donatella, and Sidney Tarrow. 2005. *Transnational Protest and Global Activism.* Lanham, MD: Rowman & Littlefield Publishers.

Democracy Now. 2009. "Video of Reclaim Power Demonstration." Transcribed by author. Available online at: http://www.democracynow.org/2009/12/16/headlines#1. Retrieved January 22, 2010.

Diani, Mario. 1995. *Green Networks: A Structural Analysis of the Italian Environmental Movement, Environment, Politics and Society Series.* Edinburgh: Edinburgh University Press.

2003. "Networks and Social Movements: A Research Program." In *Social Movements and Networks: Relational Approaches to Collective Action*, edited by Mario Diani and Doug McAdam. Oxford: Oxford University Press, 299–318.

Diani, Mario, and Doug McAdam. 2003. *Social Movements and Networks: Relational Approaches to Collective Action.* New York: Oxford University Press.

Diani, Mario, Isolbel Lindsay, and Derrick Purdue. 2010. "Sustained Interactions? Social Movements and Coalitions in Local Settings." In *Social Movement Coalitions*, edited by Nella Van Dyke and Holly McCammon. Minneapolis, MN: University of Minnesota Press, 219–238.

Doherty, Brian, and Timothy Doyle. 2013. *Environmentalism, Resistance and Solidarity: The Politics of Friends of the Earth International.* New York: Palgrave Macmillan.

Dryzek, John S. 2002. *Deliberative Democracy and Beyond: Liberals, Critics, Contestations.* Oxford: Oxford University Press.

Durban Group for Climate Justice. 2005. "The Durban Declaration on Carbon Trading." Available online at: www.durbanclimatejustice. org/durban-declaration/english.html. Retrieved May 10, 2014.

Duwe, Matthias. 2001. "The Climate Action Network: A Glance Behind the Curtains of a Transnational NGO Network." *Review of European Community & International Environmental Law* 10 (2): 177–189.

Earl, Jennifer, Andrew Martin, John D. McCarthy, and Sarah A. Soule. 2004. "The Use of Newspaper Data in the Study of Collective Action." *Annual Review of Sociology* 30 (1): 65–80.

Earth Negotiations Bulletin. 2011. "Summary of the Durban Climate Change Conference." *Earth Negotiations Bulletin* 12 (534): 1–34.

Edelman, Marc. 2009. "Peasant–farmer Movements, Third World Peoples, and the Seattle Protests against the World Trade Organization, 1999." *Dialectical Anthropology* 33 (2): 109–128.

Edwards, Bob, and John D McCarthy. 2004. "Resources and Social Movement Mobilization." In *The Blackwell Companion to Social Movements*, edited by David A. Snow, Sarah A. Soule and Hanspeter Kriesi. Oxford: Blackwell Publishing, 116–151.

Edwards, Bob, Michael W. Foley, and Mario Diani. 2001. *Beyond Tocqueville: Civil Society and the Social Capital Debate in Comparative Perspective.* London: University Press of New England.

Edwards, Michael. 2008. *Just Another Emperor? The Rise of Philanthrocapitalism.* New York: Demos.

Eisinger, P. 1973. "The Conditions of Protest Behavior in American Cities." *American Political Science Review* 81 (1): 11–28.

Emirbayer, M. 1997. "Manifesto for a Relational Society." *American Journal of Sociology* 103 (2): 281–317.

Emirbayer, Mustafa, and Jeff Goodwin. 1994. "Network Analysis, Culture, and the Problem of Agency." *American Journal of Sociology* 99 (6): 1411–1454.

Emirbayer, Mustafa, and Mimi Sheller. 1999. "Publics in History." *Theory and Society* 28 (1): 145–197.

Epstein, Charlotte. 2008. *The Power of Words in International Relations: Birth of an Anti-Whaling Discourse*. Cambridge, MA: MIT Press.

Fisher, Dana R. 2004. "Civil Society Protest and Participation: Civic Engagement Within the Multilateral Governance Regime." In *Emerging Forces in Environmental Governance*, edited by Kanie Norichicka and Peter Haas. Tokyo: United Nations University Press, 176–199.

2010. "COP 15 in Copenhagen: How the Merging of Movements Left Civil Society Out in the Cold." *Global Environmental Politics* 10 (2): 11–18.

Florini, Ann. 2000. *The Third Force: The Rise of Transnational Civil Society*. Tokyo: Carnegie Endowment for International Peace.

2005. *The Coming Democracy: New Rules for Running the World*. Washington: Brookings Institution Press.

Fowler, James H., Michael T. Heaney, David W. Nickerson, John F. Padgett, and Betsy Sinclair. 2011. "Causality in Social Networks." *American Politics Research* 39 (2): 437–480.

Friedman, Elisabeth Jay, Kathryn Hochstetler, and Ann Marie Clark. 2005. *Sovereignty, Democracy, and Global Civil Society: State-Society Relations at UN World Conferences*. Albany: State University of New York Press.

Friedman, Lisa. 2009. "Some Climate Experts Seek Alternatives to the UN Process." *The New York Times*. Available online at: www.nytimes.com/cwire/2009/12/21/21climatewire-some-climate-experts-seek-alternative-to-un-p-5632.html?pagewanted=all. Retrieved May 12, 2014.

2010. "A Near-Consensus Keeps UN Climate Process Alive and Moving Ahead." *The New York Times*. Available online at: www.nytimes.com/cwire/2010/12/13/13climatewire-a-near-consen-sus-decision-keeps-un-climate-p-77618.html?scp=12&sq=bolivia%20climate&st=cse. Retrieved May 12, 2014.

Friends of the Earth International. 2009. "Copenhagen: A Disaster for the World's Poorest." Available online at: www.foei.org/en/media/archive/2009/copenhagen-a-disaster-for-the-worlds-poorest. Retrieved May 12, 2014.

Gamson, William A. 1992. *Talking Politics*. Cambridge: Cambridge University Press.

Givan, Rebecca Kolins, Kenneth Roberts, and Sarah A. Soule. 2010. *The Diffusion of Social Movements: Actors, Mechanisms, and Political Effects*. Cambridge: Cambridge University Press.

Goldtooth, Tom. 2010. Interview transcript with Tom Goldtooth from Democracy Now!, December 9, 2010. Available online at : www.democracynow.org/2010/12/9/prominent_indigenous_environmental_activist_blocked_from. Retrieved May 10, 2014.

Goodwin, Jeff, and James M. Jasper. 2004. *Rethinking Social Movements: Structure, Meaning, and Emotion, People, Passions, and Power*. Lanham, MD: Rowman & Littlefield Publishers.

Gould, Roger V., and Roberto M. Fernandez. 1989. "Structures of Mediation: A Formal Approach to Brokerage in Transaction Networks." *Sociological Methodology* 19 (1): 89–126.

Granovetter, Mark S. 1973. "The Strength of Weak Ties." *American Journal of Sociology* 78 (6): 1360–1380.

1978. "Threshold Models of Collective Behavior." *American Journal of Sociology* 83 (6): 420–443.

1985. "Economic Action and Social Structure: The Problem of Embeddedness." *American Journal of Sociology* 91 (3): 481–510.

Greenpeace International. 2009. "Copenhagen Climate Summit: Greenpeace Demands." Available online at: www.greenpeace.org/international/Global/international/planet-2/report/2009/5/copenhagen-greenpeace-demands.pdf. Retrieved May 20, 2014.

Guggenheim, Davis. 2006. *An Inconvenient Truth* (film). Lawrence Bender Productions and Participant Media.

Gulbrandsen, Lars H., and Steinar Andresen. 2004. "NGO Influence in the Implementation of the Kyoto Protocol: Compliance, Flexibility Mechanisms, and Sinks." *Global Environmental Politics* 4 (4): 54–75.

Gupta, Dev. 2003. "Radical Flank Effects: The Effect of Radical-Moderate Splits in Regional Nationalist Movements." Working Paper, Program for the Study of Contentious Politics, Cornell University.

Hadden, Jennifer. 2014. "Explaining Variation in Transnational Climate Change Activism: The Role of Inter-Movement Spillover." *Global Environmental Politics* 14 (2): 7–25.

Hadden, Jennifer, and Sidney Tarrow. 2007. "Spillover or Spillout? The Global Justice Movement in the United States After 9/11." *Mobilization* 12 (4): 359–376.

Hafner-Burton, Emilie M., Miles Kahler, and Alexander H. Montgomery. 2009. "Network Analysis for International Relations." *International Organization* 63 (3): 559–592.

Haines, Herbert H. 1984. "Black Radicalization and the Funding of Civil Rights: 1957–1970." *Social Problems* 32 (1): 31–43.

Hannan, Michael T., and Glenn Carroll. 1992. *Dynamics of Organizational Populations: Density, Legitimation, and Competition.* New York: Oxford University Press.

Hannan, Michael T., James N. Baron, Greta Hsu, and Ozegan Koçak. 2006. "Organizational Identities and the Hazard of Change." *Industrial and Corporate Change* 15 (5): 755–784.

Hannan, Michael T., and John Freeman. 1987. "The Ecology of Organizational Founding: American Labor Unions, 1836–1985." *American Journal of Sociology* 92 (4): 910–943.

Hansen, James. 2009. "Interview with James Hansen for *Democracy Now!*" Available online at: www.democracynow.org/2009/12/22/leading_climate_scientist_james_hansen_on. Retrieved May 23, 2014.

Hari, Johann. 2010. "The Wrong Kind of Green." *The Nation.* Available online at: www.thenation.com/article/wrong-kind-green#. Retrieved May 10, 2014.

Haveman, Heather A., and Hayagreeba Rao. 1997. "Structuring a Theory of Moral Sentiments: Institutional and Organizational Coevolution in the Early Thrift Industry." *American Journal of Sociology* 102 (6): 1606–1651.

Heaney, Michael T., and Fabio Rojas. 2014. "Hybrid Activism: Social Movement Mobilization in a Multimovement Environment." *American Journal of Sociology* 11 (4): 1047–1103.

2015. *Party in the Street: The Antiwar Movement and the Democratic Party after 9/11.* New York: Cambridge University Press.

Hernández, Esteban Lazo. 2009. Transcribed from video recording of UNFCCC floor speech December 17, 2009. Available online at: http://unfccc2.meta-fusion.com/kongresse/cop15_hls/templ/play.php?id_kongresssession=4205. Retrieved January 15, 2011.

Hertel, Shareen. 2006. *Unexpected Power: Conflict and Change Among Transnational Activists.* Ithaca, NY: Cornell University Press.

Higgott, Richard A., Geoffrey R.D. Underhill, and Andreas Bieler. 2000. *Non-State Actors and Authority in the Global System.* London: Routledge.

Hoffman, Matthew. 2008. "Where the States Are: Environmental NGOs and the UN Climate Negotiations." In *Transnational Activism in the UN and EU: A Comparative Study,* edited by Jutta M. Joachim and Birgit Locher. New York: Taylor and Francis, 29–43.

Hosmer, David W., and Stanley Lemeshow. 2000. *Applied Logistic Regression.* New York: John Wiley & Sons.

Imig, Douglas R., and Sidney G. Tarrow. 2001. *Contentious Europeans: Protest and Politics in an Emerging Polity, Governance in Europe.* Lanham, MD: Rowman & Littlefield.

INCITE! Women of Color Against Violence. 2007. *The Revolution Will Not be Funded: Beyond the Non-Profit Industrial Complex.* Cambridge, MA: South End Press.

Ingram, Paul. 2002. "Interorganizational Learning." In *The Blackwell Companion to Organizations*, edited by J.C. Baum. Oxford: Blackwell, 624–663.

Intergovernmental Panel on Climate Change. 2007. *Fourth Assessment Report.* Geneva: United Nations Intergovernmental Panel on Climate Change.

2013. *Fifth Assessment Report.* Geneva: United Nations Intergovernmental Panel on Climate Change.

Jacobs, Michael. 2012. "The Doha Climate Talks Were a Start, but 2015 Will Be the Moment of Truth." *The Guardian.* Available online at: www.guardian.co.uk/commentisfree/2012/dec/10/doha-climate-talks-global-warming. Retrieved May 10, 2014.

Janssen, Marco A., Orian Bodin, and John M. Anderies. 2006. "Toward a Network Perspective of the Study of Resilience in Social-Ecological Systems." *Ecology and Society* 11 (1): 15 [online]. Available at: www.ecologyandsociety.org/vol11/iss1/art15/

Javeline, Debra. 2014. "The Most Important Topic Political Scientists Are Not Studying: Adapting to Climate Change." *Perspectives on Politics.* Available at DOI: http://dx.doi.org/10.1017/S1537592714000784

Jinnah, Sikina. 2011. "Climate Change Bandwagoning: The Impacts of Strategic Linkages on Regime Design, Maintenance, and Death." *Global Environmental Politics* 11 (3): 1–9.

Joachim, Jutta M, and Birgit Locher. 2008. *Transnational Activism in the UN and EU: A Comparative Study.* New York: Taylor and Francis.

Johnson, Rebecca. 1999. "Advocates and Activists: Conflicting Approaches on Nonproliferation and the Test Ban Treaty." In *The Third Force: The Rise of Transnational Civil Society*, edited by Ann Florini. Washington, DC: The Carnegie Endowment for International Peace, 49–81.

Juris, Jeffrey S. 2008. *Networking Futures: The Movements against Corporate Globalization, Experimental futures.* Durham, NC: Duke University Press.

Kahler, Miles. 2009. *Networked Politics: Agency, Power, and Governance, Cornell Studies in Political Economy.* Ithaca, NY: Cornell University Press.

Keck, Margaret E., and Kathryn Sikkink. 1998. *Activists Beyond Borders: Advocacy Networks in International Politics.* Ithaca, NY: Cornell University Press.

Keohane, Robert O., and David G. Victor. 2011. "The Regime Complex for Climate Change." *Perspectives on Politics* 9 (1): 7–23.

Khagram, Sanjeev. 2004. *Dams and Development: Transnational Struggles for Water and Power*. Ithaca, NY: Cornell University Press.

Khagram, Sanjeev, James V. Riker, and Kathryn Sikkink. 2002. *Restructuring World Politics: Transnational Social Movements, Networks, And Norms*. Minneapolis: University of Minnesota Press.

Khor, Martin. 2009. "Blame Denmark, not China, for Copenhagen Failure." *The Guardian*. Available online at: www.theguardian.com/commentisfree/cif-green/2009/dec/28/copenhagen-denmark-china. Retrieved May 23, 2014.

Kitschelt, Herbert P. 1986. "Political Opportunity Structures and Political Protest: Anti-Nuclear Movements in Four Democracies." *British Journal of Political Science* 16 (1): 57–85.

Klandermans, Bert. 1990. "Linking the 'New' and the 'Old': Movement Networks in the Netherlands." In *Challenging the Political Order: New Social and Political Movements in Western Democracies*, edited by Russell J. Dalton and Manfred Kuechler. New York: Oxford University Press, 122–136.

Klein, Naomi. 2009. "The Seattle Activists' Coming of Age in Copenhagen Will Be Very Disobedient." *The Guardian*. Available online at: www.theguardian.com/commentisfree/cifamerica/2009/nov/12/seattle-coming-age-disobedient-copenhagen. Retrieved May 23, 2014.

Klimaforum. 2009. "People's Declaration." Available online at: http://declaration.klimaforum.org/files/declaration/declaration_screen.pdf. Retrieved January 23, 2011.

Kollman, Ken. 1998. *Outside Lobbying: Public Opinion and Interest Group Strategies*. Princeton, NJ: Princeton University Press.

Koopmans, Ruud. 1995. *Democracy From Below: New Social Movements And The Political System In West Germany*. Boulder, CO: Westview Press.

2002. "Codebook for the Analysis of Political Mobilisation and Communication in European Public Spheres." Available online at: http://europub.wzb.eu/Data/Codebooks%20questionnaires/D2-1-claims-codebook.pdf. Retrieved May 10, 2014.

Koopmans, Ruud, and Dieter Rucht. 2002. "Protest Event Analysis." In *Methods of Social Movement Research*, edited by Bert Klandermans and Suzanne Staggenborg. Minneapolis: University of Minnesota Press, 231–259.

Kriesi, Hanspeter. 2007. "Interview Questionnaire for Interviews with Collective Actors in Claims-making and Political Mobilization." Available online at: http://europub.wzb.eu/Data/Codebooks%20questionnaires/WP5/Qfinal-WP5-EUintegration.pdf. Retrieved May 10, 2014.

Lecy, Jesse D., George E. Mitchell, and Hans Peter Schmitz. 2010. "Advocacy Organizations, Networks, and the Firm Analogy." In *Advocacy Organizations and Collective Action*, edited by Aseem Prakash and Mary Kay Gugerty. New York: Cambridge University Press, 205–228.

Lee, John. 2009. "How China Stiffed the World in Copenhagen." *Foreign Policy*. Available online at: www.foreignpolicy.com/articles/2009/12/21/how_china_stiffed_the_world_in_copenhagen. Retrieved May 23, 2014.

Levi, Margaret, and Gillian H. Murphy. 2006. "Coalitions of Contention: The Case of the WTO Protests in Seattle." *Political Studies* 54 (3): 651–670.

Lin, Nan. 2001. *Social Capital: A Theory of Social Structure and Action, Structural Analysis in the Social Sciences*. New York: Cambridge University Press.

Lipschutz, Ronnie D. 1992. "Reconstructing World Politics: The Emergence of Global Civil Society." *Millennium – Journal of International Studies* 21 (3): 389–420.

Long, J. Scott, and Jeremy Freese. 2006. *Regression Models for Categorical Dependent Variables Using Stata*. College Station, TX: StataCorp LP.

Lyans, Mark. 2009. "How do I know China Wrecked the Copenhagen Deal? I Was In the Room." *The Guardian*. Available online at: www.theguardian.com/environment/2009/dec/22/copenhagen-climate-change-mark-lynas. Retrived May 23, 2014.

Mahoney, Christine. 2008. *Brussels versus the Beltway: Advocacy in the United States and the European Union*. Washington, DC: Georgetown University Press.

Maney, Gregory M. 2001. "Rival Transnational Networks and Indigenous Rights: The San Blas Kuna in Panama and the Yanomami in Brazil." In *Political Opportunities Social Movements, and Democratization Research in Social Movements, Conflicts and Change*, edited by Patrick G. Coy. New York: Emerald Publishing Group Limited, 103–144.

Marks, Gary, and Doug McAdam. 1999. "On the Relationship of Political Opportunities to the Form of Collective Action: The Case of the European Union." In *Social Movements in a Globalizing World*, edited by Donatella della Porta, Hanspeter Kriesi and Dieter Rucht. New York: St. Martin's Press, 97–111.

Marsden, Peter V. 1983. "Restricted Access in Networks and Models of Power." *American Journal of Sociology* 88 (3): 686–717.

Matthews, Jessica. 1997. "Power Shift." *Foreign Affairs* 76 (1): 50–66.

Mayhew, Bruce H., and Roger L. Levinger. 1976. "Size and the Density of Interaction in Human Aggregates." *American Journal of Sociology* 82 (1): 86–110.

McAdam, Doug. 1995. "'Initiator' and 'Spin-off' Movements: Diffusion Processes in Protest Cycles." In *Repertoires and Cycles of Collective Action*, edited by Mark Traugott. Durham, NC: Duke University Press, 217–240.

    1999. *Political Process and the Development of Black Insurgency, 1930–1970*. Chicago, IL: University of Chicago Press.

    2003. "Beyond Structural Analysis: Toward a More Dynamic Understanding of Social Movements." In *Social Movements and Networks: Relational Approaches to Collective Action*, edited by Mario Diani and Doug McAdam. New York: Oxford University Press, 281–298.

McAdam, Doug, John D. McCarthy, and Mayer N. Zald. 1988. "Social Movements." In *Handbook of Sociology*, edited by Neil Smelser. Beverly Hills, CA: Sage, 695–737.

McAdam, Doug, Sidney Tarrow, and Charles Tilly. 2001. *Dynamics of Contention. Cambridge Studies in Contentious Politics*. New York: Cambridge University Press.

McCammon, Holly J., and Nella Van Dyke. 2010. *Social Movement Coalitions*. Minneapolis: University of Minnesota Press.

McCammon, Holly J., Karen E. Campbell, Ellen M. Granberg, and Christine Mowery. 2001. "How Movements Win: Gendered Opportunity Structures and U.S. Women's Suffrage Movements, 1866 to 1919." *American Sociological Review* 66 (1): 49–70.

McCarthy, John D., and Mayer N. Zald. 1973. *The Trend of Social Movements in America: Professionalization and Resource Mobilization*. Morristown, NJ: General Learning Press.

    1977. "Resource Mobilization and Social Movements: A Partial Theory." *American Journal of Sociology* 82 (6): 1212–1241.

McGregor, Ian M. 2010. "Disenfranchisement of Countries and Civil Society at COP-15 in Copenhagen." *Global Environmental Politics* 11 (1): 1–7.

McKibben, Bill. 2009. "With Climate Agreement, Obama Guts Progressive Values, Argues McKibben." *Grist Magazine*. Available online at: http://grist.org/article/2009-12-18-with-climate-agreement-obama-guts-progressive-values/. Retrieved May 23, 2014.

McPherson, Miller, Lynn Lovin, and James Cook. 2001. "Birds of a Feather: Homophily in Social Networks." *Annual Review of Sociology* 27 (1): 415–444.

Meilstrup, Per. 2010. "The Runaway Summit: The Background Story of the Danish Presidency of COP15, the UN Climate Change Conference." In *Danish Foreign Policy Yearbook*, edited by Nanna Hvidt and Hans Mouritzen. Copenhagen: DIIS Book, 113–135.

Meyer, David S. 1993. "Peace Protest and Policy." *Policy Studies Journal* 21 (1): 35–51.

Meyer, David S. 2004. "Protest and Political Opportunities." *Annual Review of Sociology* 30 (1): 125–145.

Meyer, David S., and Debra C. Minkoff. 2004. "Conceptualizing Political Opportunity." *Social Forces* 82 (4): 1457–1492.

Meyer, David S., and Nancy Whittier. 1994. "Social Movement Spillover." *Social Problems* 41 (2): 277–298.

Michels, Robert. 1958. *Political Parties.* Glencoe, IL: The Free Press.

Minkoff, Debra C. 1994. "From Service Provision to Institutional Advocacy: The Shifting Legitimacy of Organizational Forms." *Social Forces* 72 (4): 943–969.

Mische, Ann. 2003. "Cross-Talk in Movements: Rethinking the Culture-Network Link." In *Social Movements and Networks: Relational Approaches to Collective Action,* edited by Mario Diani and Doug McAdam. Oxford: Oxford University Press, 258–280.

Mische, Ann. 2010. "Relational Sociology, Culture and Agency." In *Sage Handbook of Social Network Analysis,* edited by John Scott and Peter J. Carrington. Thousand Oaks, CA: Sage, 80–97.

Monbiot, George. 2009. "Requiem for a Crowded Planet." *The Guardian.* Available online at: www.monbiot.com/2009/12/21/requiem-for-a-crowded-planet/. Retrieved May 23, 2014.

Morales, Evo. 2009. Transcribed from author's field notes from open meeting at Klimaforum, December 17, 2009.

        2010. "Speech at the International Peoples Summit on Climate Change, Cochabamba, Bolivia, April 20, 2010." Available online at: http://alainet.org/active/37560. Retrieved September 15, 2010.

Müller, Tadzio. 2008. "The Movement Is Dead, Long Live the Movement." *Turbulence Magazine.* Available online at: http://turbulence.org.uk/turbulence-4/the-movement-is-dead-long-live-the-movement/. Retrieved January 31, 2010.

Murdie, Amanda. 2014. "The Ties that Bind: A Network Analysis of Human Rights International Nongovernmental Organizations." *British Journal of Political Science* 44 (1): 1–27.

Murdie, Amanda M., and David R. Davis. 2011. "Shaming and Blaming: Using Events Data to Assess the Impact of Human Rights INGOs." *International Studies Quarterly* 56 (1): 1–16.

Nelson, Paul J. 2002. "Agendas, Accountability and Legitimacy among Transnational Networks Lobbying the World Bank." In *Restructuring World Politics: Transnational Social Movements, Networks and Norms,* edited by Sanjeev Khagram, James V. Riker and Kathryn Sikkink. Minneapolis, MN: University of Minnesota Press, 131–154.

Newell, Peter. 2000. *Climate for Change: Non-State Actors and the Global Politics of the Greenhouse.* Cambridge: Cambridge University Press.

Nobel Prize Committee. 2007. "Award Ceremony Speech." Available online at: www.nobelprize.org/nobel_prizes/peace/laureates/2007/presentation-speech.html. Retrieved May 10, 2014.

O'Neill, Kate. 2004. "Transnational Protest: State, Circuses, and Conflict at the Frontline of Global Politics." *International Studies Review* 6 (2): 233–251.

O'Neill, Kate, and Stacy VanDeveer. 2005. "Transnational Environmental Activism after Seattle: Between Emancipation and Arrogance." In *Charting Transnational Democracy: Beyond Global Arrogance*, edited by Janie Leatherman and Julie Webber. New York: Palgrave Macmillan, 195–220.

Oliver, Pamela, and Gerald Marwell. 1988. "The Paradox of Group Size in Collective Action. A Theory of the Critical Mass II." *American Sociological Review* 53 (1): 1–8.

Olson, Mancur. 1965. *Logic of Collective Action*. Cambridge, MA: Harvard University Press.

Ostrom, Elinor. 1990. *Governing the Commons*. New York: Cambridge University Press.

Peterson, M.J. 1992. "Whalers, Cetologists, Environmentalists and the International Management of Whaling." *International Organization* 46 (1): 147–186.

Pew Center on Global Climate Change. 2011. "Common Metrics: Comparing Countries' Climate Pledges." Available online at: www.c2es.org/docUploads/country-pledge-brief.pdf. Retrieved April 1, 2014.

Pfeffer, Jeffrey, and Gerald R. Salancik. 1978. *The External Control of Organizations: A Resource Dependence Perspective*. New York: Harper & Row.

Piven, Frances Fox, and Richard A. Cloward. 1977. *Poor People's Movements: Why They Succeed, How They Fail*. New York: Vintage Books.

Pleyers, Geoffrey. 2010. *Alter-Globalization: Becoming Actors in the Global Age*. Cambridge: Polity.

Polletta, Francesca. 2002. *Freedom Is an Endless Meeting: Democracy in American Social Movements*. Chicago: University of Chicago Press.

Polos, Laszlo, Michael T. Hannan, and Glenn R. Carroll. 2002. "Foundations of a Theory of Social Forms." *Industrial Corporate Change* 1(1): 85–115.

Portes, Alejandro, and Patricia Landolt. 1996. "The Downside of Social Capital." *The American Prospect* 7 (26): 18–21.

Prakash, Aseem, and Mary Kay Gugerty. 2010. *Advocacy Organizations and Collective Action*. New York: Cambridge University Press.

Price, Richard MacKay. 2003. "Transnational Civil Society and Advocacy in World Politics." *World Politics* 55 (4): 579–606.

210   *References*

Princen, Thomas, and Matthias Finger. 1994. *Environmental NGOs in World Politics: Linking the Local and the Global.* New York: Routledge.

Putnam, Robert D. 2000. *Bowling Alone: the Collapse and Revival of American Community.* New York: Simon & Schuster.

Rahman, Atiq, and Annie Roncerel. 1994. "A View from the Ground Up." In *Negotiating Climate Change: The Inside Story of the Rio Convention,* edited by Irving M. Mintzer and J. Amber Leonard. Cambridge: Cambridge University Press, 239–273.

Rapp, Tobias, Christian Schwägerl, and Gerald Traufetter. 2010. "How China and India Sabotaged the UN Climate Summit." *Spiegel Online.* Available online at: www.spiegel.de/international/world/the-copenhagen-protocol-how-china-and-india-sabotaged-the-un-climate-summit-a-692861.html. Retrieved June 1, 2010.

Reinicke, Wolfgang H. 2000. "The Other World Wide Web: Global Public Policy Networks." *Foreign Policy* (117): 44–57.

Reitan, Ruth. 2007. *Global Activism.* London: Routledge.

2010. "Coordinated Power in Contemporary Leftist Activism." In *Power and Global Activism,* edited by Thomas Olesen. London: Routledge, 51–71.

Risse, Thomas, Stephen C. Ropp, and Kathryn Sikkink. 1999. *The Power of Human Rights: International Norms and Domestic Change.* New York: Cambridge University Press.

Rogers, Everett. 1995. *The Diffusion of Innovations.* New York: Free Press.

Rohrschneider, Robert, and Russel J. Dalton. 2002. "A Global Network? Transnational Cooperation among Environmental Groups." *The Journal of Politics* 64 (2): 510–533.

Rootes, Christopher. 2003. *Environmental Protest in Western Europe.* Oxford: Oxford University Press.

Rootes, Christopher. 2012. "New Issues, New Forms of Action? Climate Change and Environmental Activism in Britain." In *New Participatory Dimensions in Civil Society: Professionalization and Individualized Collective Action,* edited by Jan W. van Deth and William Maloney. London: Routledge, 46–68.

Rucht, Dieter. 1989. "Environmental Movement Organizations in West Germany and France." In *Organizing for Change,* edited by Bert Klandermans. Greenwich, CT: JAI Press, 61–94.

1990. "The Strategies and Action Repertoires of New Movements." In *Challenging the Political Order,* edited by Russell Dalton and Manfred Kuechler. New York: Oxford University Press, 156–175.

Sarewitz, Daniel, and Roger Pielke. 2000. "Breaking the Global-Warming Gridlock." *The Atlantic Monthly.* Available online at:

www.theatlantic.com/magazine/archive/2000/07/breaking-the-global-warming-gridlock/304973/. Retrieved January 20, 2014.

Saunders, Clare. 2007. "Using Social Network Analysis to Explore Social Movements: A Relational Approach." *Social Movement Studies* 6 (3): 227–243.

Schlozman, Kay Lehman, and John T. Tierney. 1986. *Organized Interests and American Democracy*. New York: Harper & Row.

Scholte, Jan Aart. 2002. "Civil Society and Democracy in Global Governance." *Global Governance* 8 (1): 281–304.

Scholte, Jan Aart, and Albrecht Schnabel. 2002. *Civil Society and Global Finance*. New York: Routledge.

Schroeder, Heike, Maxwell T. Boykoff, and Laura Spiers. 2012. "Equity and State Representations in Climate Negotiations." *Nature* 2 (12): 834–836.

Schroeder, Heike, and Heather Lovell. 2012. "The Role of Non-Nation-State Actors and Side Events in the International Climate Negotiations." *Climate Policy* 12 (1): 23–37.

Scott, W. Richard, Martin Ruef, Peter J. Medel, and Carol A. Caronna. 1999. *Institutional Change and Healthcare Organizations*. Chicago, IL: University of Chicago Press.

Sikkink, Kathryn. 2009. "The Power of Networks in International Politics." In *Networked Politics: Agency, Power, and Governance*, edited by Miles Kahler. Ithaca, NY: Cornell University Press, 228–247.

Smith, Jackie. 2001. "The Battle of Seattle and the Future of Social Movements." *Mobilization* 6 (1): 1–21.

2008. *Social Movements for Global Democracy*. Baltimore, MD: Johns Hopkins University Press.

Smith, Jackie, Marina Karides, Marc Becker, Dorval Brunelle, Christopher Chase-Dunn, Rosalba Icaza, Jeffrey Juris, Lorenzo Mosca, Donatella della Porta, Ellen Reese, PeterJay Smith, and Rolando Vászuez. 2007. *The World Social Forums and the Challenge of Global Democracy*. Boulder, CO: Paradigm Press.

Smith, Jackie, and Dawn Wiest. 2012. *Social Movements in the World-System: The Politics of Crisis and Transformation*. New York: Russell Sage Foundation.

Snow, David A., and Robert D. Benford. 1988. "Ideology, Frame Resonance and Participant Mobilization." In *From Structure to Action*, edited by Bert Klandemans, Hanspeter Kriesi, and Sidney Tarrow. Greenwich, CT: JAI Press, 197–218.

Snow, David A., Sarah A. Soule, and Daniel M. Cress. 2005. "Identifying the Precipitants of Homeless Protest across 17 U.S. Cities, 1980 to 1990." *Social Forces* 83 (3): 1183–1210.

Soule, Sarah A. 1997. "The Student Divestment Movement in the United States and Tactical Diffusion: The Shantytown Protest." *Social Forces* 75 (3): 855–882.

2004. "Diffusion Processes Within and Across Movements." In *The Blackwell Companion to Social Movements*, edited by David Snow, Sarah Soule, and Hanspeter Kriesi. Oxford: Blackwell Publishing, 294–310.

Staggenborg, Suzanne. 1986. "Coalition Work in the Pro-Choice Movement: Organizational and Environmental Opportunities and Obstacles." *Social Problems* 33 (5): 374–390.

1988. "The Consequences of Professionalization and Formalization in the Pro-Choice Movement." *American Sociological Review* 53 (4): 585–605.

Stern, Todd. 2013. "The Shape of a New International Climate Agreement." Available online at: www.state.gov/e/oes/rls/remarks/2013/215720.htm. Retrieved May 23, 2014.

Stevenson, Hayley, and John S. Dryzek. 2012. "The Discursive Democratization of Global Climate Governance." *Environmental Politics* 21 (2): 189–210.

Stovel, Katherine, and Lynette Shaw. 2012. "Brokerage." *Annual Review of Sociology* 38: 139–158.

Stroup, Sarah. 2012. *Borders Among Activists: International NGOs in the United States, Britain and France*. Ithaca, NY: Cornell University Press.

Tarrow, Sidney. 1989. *Democracy and Disorder: Protest and Politics in Italy, 1965–1975*. Oxford: Oxford University Press.

2005a. "The Dualities of Transnational Contention: 'Two Activist Solitudes' or a New World Altogether?" *Mobilization* 10 (1): 53–72.

2005b. *The New Transnational Activism*. New York: Cambridge University Press.

2011. *Power in Movement*. New York: Cambridge University Press.

Taylor, Verta, and Nancy Whittier. 1993. "Collective Identity in Social Movement Communities: Lesbian Feminist Mobilization." In *Frontiers in Social Movement Theory*, edited by Aldon D. Morris and Carol McClurg Mueller. New Haven: Yale University Press, 104–129.

Tilly, Charles. 1978. *From Mobilization to Revolution*. New York: Addison-Wesley.

1995. *Popular Contention in Great Britain, 1758–1834*. Cambridge, MA: Harvard University Press.

Tokar, Brian. 2010. *Towards Climate Justice*. Porsgrunn, Norway: Communalism Press.

Uba, Katrin, and Fredrik Uggla. 2011. "Protest Actions against the European Union, 1992–2007." *West European Politics* 34 (2): 384–393.

United Nations Economic Commission for Europe. 2010. "Promoting the Principles of the Aarhus Convention in the Lead Up to, During and After the United Nations Climate Change Conference 2009, Copenhagen." Available online at: http://unfccc.int/resource/docs/2010/smsn/igo/o88.pdf. Retrieved May 20, 2014.

United Nations Framework Convention on Climate Change. 1992. "Framework Convention on Climate Change." Available online at: http://unfccc.int/essential_background/convention/background/items/2853.php. Retrieved May 20, 2014.

1997. "Kyoto Protocol." Available online at: http://unfccc.int/kyoto_protocol/items/2830.php. Retrieved May 20, 2014.

2007. "Bali Action Plan Text." Available online at: http://unfccc.int/resource/docs/2007/cop13/eng/06a01.pdf. Retrieved May 20, 2014.

2009a. "Copenhagen Accord." Available online at: http://unfccc.int/resource/docs/2009/cop15/eng/11a01.pdf. Retrieved May 20, 2014.

2009b. "Video recording of Delibrations during COP 15." Available online at: http://www1.cop15.meta-fusion.com/kongresse/cop15/templ/play.php?id_kongressmain=1&theme=unfccc&id_kongress-session=2755 and http://cop15.meta-fusion.com/kongresse/cop15/templ/play.php?id_kongresssession=2761&theme=unfccc. Retrieved May 20, 2014.

2010. "Guidelines for the Participation of Representatives of Non-governmental Organizations at Meetings of the Bodies of the United Nations Framework Convention on Climate Change." Available online at: http://unfccc.int/parties_and_observers/ngo/items/3667.php. Retrieved May 20, 2014.

2011a. "Durban Platform." Available online at: http://unfccc.int/files/meetings/durban_nov_2011/decisions/application/pdf/cop17_dur-banplatform.pdf. Retrieved May 23. 2014.

2011b. "Report on the In-session Workshop to Further Develop Ways to Enhance the Engagement of Observer Organizations: Notes From the Chair." Available online at: http://unfccc.int/documenta-tion/documents/advanced_search/items/6911.php?priref=600006319. Retrieved May 20, 2014.

2013. "Civil Society and the Climate Change Process: Participation Report." Available online at: http://unfccc.int/files/parties_and_ob-servers/ngo/application/pdf/cumulative_admissions_of_observer_organizations_cop_1-18_updated_14.12.12.pdf. Retrieved May 20, 2014.

Unmussig, Barbara. 2011. "NGOs and Climate Crisis: Fragmentation, Lines of Conflict and Strategic Approaches." Available online at: http://www.boell.de/ecology/society/ecology-society-ngos-climate-crisis-12261.html. Retrieved May 20, 2014.

Unsigned Movement Document. 2009. "Why Climate Change is Not An Environmental Issue." Available online at: http://notenvironmental. blogspot.com/. Retrieved June 10, 2014.

Van der Zee, Bibi. 2009a. "An Activist's Guide to Copenhagen." *The Guardian*. Available online at: www.guardian.co.uk/environment/ blog/2009/nov/12/copenhagen-activists-climate-change. Retrieved May 20, 2014.

2009b. "Danish Police Raid Copenhagen Climate Campaigners' Rooms." *The Guardian*. Available online at: www.theguardian. com/environment/2009/dec/09/danish-police-raid-climate-campaigner-rooms. Retrieved June 20, 2014.

Van Dyke, Nella. 2003. "Crossing Movement Boundaries: Factors that Facilitate Coalition Protest by American College Students, 1930–1990." *Social Problems* 50 (2): 226–250.

Victor, David. 2011. *Global Warming Gridlock: Creating More Effective Strategies for Protecting the Planet*. New York: Cambridge University Press.

Vidal, John. 2009. "Rich and Poor Countries Blame Each Other for Failure of Copenhagen Deal." *The Guardian*. Available online at: www.theguardian.com/environment/2009/dec/19/copenhagen-blame-game. Retrieved May 23, 2014.

Wahlstrom, Mattias, Magnus Wennerhag, and Christopher Rootes. 2013. "Framing 'The Climate Issue': Patterns of Participation and Prognostic Frames Among Climate Summit Protestors." *Global Environmental Politics* 13(4): 101–122.

Walgrave, Stefaan, Ruud Wouters, Jeroen Van Laer, Joris Verhulst, and Pauline Ketellars. 2012. "Transnational Collective Identification: May Day and Climate Change Protesters' Identification with Similar Protest Events in Other Countries." *Mobilization* 17 (3): 301–317.

Walker, Edward T., Andrew Martin, and John D. McCarthy. 2008. "Confronting the State, the Corporation and the Academy: The Influence of Institutional Targets on Social Movement Repertoires." *American Journal of Sociology* 114 (1): 35–76.

Wang, Dan J., and Sarah A. Soule. 2012. "Social Movement Organizational Collaboration: Networks of Learning and the Diffusion of Protest Tactics, 1960–1995." *American Journal of Sociology* 117 (6): 1674–1722.

Wapner, Paul. 1995. "Politics Beyond the State: Environmental Activism and World Civic Politics." *World Politics* 47 (3): 311–340.

Ward, Michael D., Katherine Stovel, and Audrey Sacks. 2011. "Network Analysis in Political Science." *Annual Review of Political Science* 14: 245–264.

Wasserman, Stanley, and Katherine Faust. 1995. *Social Network Analysis: Methods and Applications*. Cambridge: Cambridge University Press.

Willets, Peter. 1996. '*The Conscience of the World*': *The Influence of Non-Governmental Organisations in the UN System*. Washington, DC: Brookings Press.

Winship, Christopher, and Robert D. Mare. 1992. "Models for Sample Selection Bias." *Annual Review of Sociology* 18 (1): 327–350.

Wong, Wendy H. 2012. *Internal Affairs: How the Structure of NGOs Transforms Human Rights*. Ithaca, NY: Cornell University Press.

Wood, Leslie J. 2007. "Breaking the Wave: Repression, Identity and Seattle Tactics." *Mobilization* 12 (4): 377–388.

WWF International. 2009. "Global Climate Policy Position Paper." Available online at: http://awsassets.panda.org/downloads/copenhagen_expectations_paper__wwf.pdf. Retrieved May 10, 2013.

Yeo, Andrew. 2009. "Not in Anyone's Backyard: The Emergence and Identity of a Transnational Anti-Base Network." *International Studies Quarterly* 53 (3): 571–594.

Young, Iris Marion. 2000. *Inclusion and Democracy*. Oxford: Oxford University Press.

Young, Oran R. 1994. *International Governance: Protecting the Environment in a Stateless Society*. Ithaca, NY: Cornell University Press.

Zald, Mayer N. 2000. "Ideologically Structured Action." *Mobilization* 5 (1): 1–15.

Zeller, Tom Jr. 2009. "Bella Center Bulges as Climate Talks Open." *The New York Times*. Available online at: http://green.blogs.nytimes.com/2009/12/07/bella-center-bulges-as-climate-talks-open/?_php=true&_type=blogs&_r=0. Retrieved June 20, 2014.

Zeller, Tom Jr., and Lars Kroldrup. 2009. "Protesters Converge on Copenhagen." *The New York Times*. Available online at: http://www.nytimes.com/2009/12/12/world/europe/12protest.html. Retrieved June 20, 2014.

Zürn, Michael. 1998. "The Rise of International Environmental Politics: A Review of Current Research." *World Politics* 50 (4): 617–649.

Index